THE GREAT FAMILY
GETAWAY GUIDE

BILL GLEESON

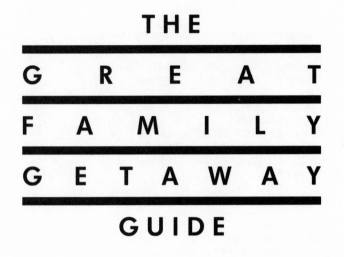

THE
GREAT
FAMILY
GETAWAY
GUIDE

Over 180 California Adventures
for You and Your Kids

Chronicle Books ■ San Francisco

Printed in the United States of America.

Library of Congress Cataloging-in-Publication Data

Gleeson, Bill.
   The great family getaway guide : over 180 California
adventures for you and your kids / Bill Gleeson.
   p.   cm.
   Includes index.
   ISBN 0-87701-413-2 (pbk.)
   1. Family recreation—California—Directories. 2. Outdoor
recreation—California—Directories. 3. Resorts—California—
Directories. 4. California—Description and travel—1981—
—Guidebooks. 1. Title.
GV182.8.G54   1988
796.5'025'794—dc19   88--4961
                                                         CIP

Editing: Carey Charlesworth
Book design: Seventeenth Street Studios
Composition: TBH/Typecast, Inc., Cotati
Cover design: Karen Pike

Photo credits

Bill Gleeson: pages xiv, 8, 12, 19, 25, 44, 47, 54, 60, 67, 76, 88, 94, 98,
      114, 116, 128, 131, 140, 147, 160, 184
The following photographs used with permission:
Alisal Guest Ranch: cover
Greenhorn Guest Ranch: page 15
The San Francisco Exploratorium: page 35, 179
San Jose Convention and Visitors Bureau: page 40
Camp Mather, Robin Lew: page 77
The Inn at Morro Bay: page 83
University of California, Santa Barbara, Vacation Center: page 90
El Encanto Hotel: page 92
Big Bear Chamber of Commerce, Celia Ralph: page 102
Queen Mary/Spruce Goose: page 106
Furnace Creek Ranch: page 112
Great America: page 133
Santa Cruz Beach Boardwalk: pages 135, 136
Six Flags Magic Mountain: page 144
Sea World: page 156
Wild Rivers: page 164
Trees of Mystery: page 168
California State Railroad Museum: page 172
Monterey Bay Aquarium: page 176

10 9 8 7 6 5 4 3 2

Chronicle Books
San Francisco, California

To Yvonne, Karin and Jeffrey

Special Thanks:
American Automobile Association
California Office of Tourism
Carey Charlesworth

Contents

I

FAMILY RESORTS AND CAMPS,
GUEST RANCHES AND
CITY ADVENTURES

II

THEME PARKS AND
BIG TIME FUN

Northern California

Southern California

III

DAYTRIPPING AND
OTHER DIVERSIONS

Introduction

During a Northern California vacation a few years ago, my wife and I, along with our three-year-old daughter, spent the night at a popular coastal inn. Unfortunately, we learned after checking in that young children were not the most welcome guests.

Undaunted, the three of us ventured brazenly into the communal parlor, our daughter's version of "Itsy Bitsy Spider" clashing with the Vivaldi concerto wafting from the stereo. We tried to interest our little soprano in a travel magazine, which was the closest thing to youthful entertainment in the house. However, her interests ran more toward building towers out of butt-laden ashtrays and playing "castle" with the hotel's delicate crystal chess pieces.

After the small one immodestly informed mom and dad (as well as several other guests within earshot) of her imminent "need to go pee-pee," we beat a hasty retreat and spent the rest of the evening as family fugitives cloistered in our room.

Sorry: No Pets or Kids

After our rites of passage into the ranks of traveling families, we began paying closer attention to the small print. Gazing at a magazine one evening I spotted an ad for an appealing retreat in the mountains. "How about this one?" I asked my wife. "Nope," she said. "It says here 'absolutely no pets or children.'"

It wasn't until I became a father that I discovered how many resort operators lump children into the pet category. (Though in truth they do share some similar habits, particularly when it comes to making messes.)

Fortunately, there are resorts that not only tolerate but welcome our kind, and we soon began picking up family vacation tips from other young parents. It wasn't long before we had quite a list of possibilities.

Fort Trinity is designed for the exclusive use of the under-four-foot set.

There's the guest ranch that takes guests on old-fashioned hay rides, the museum that lets kids pet a live starfish, the coastal resort with its own ocean-view miniature golf course, the children's park with play equipment designed by the creator of "Dennis the Menace" and the mountain resort whose activities include rock-sliding down waterfalls.

The destinations described in the following pages meet one important criterion. They not only "accept" children but treat youngsters as real people. That means offering–in addition to adult-oriented activities–special facilities and/or services that children can enjoy.

While these activities traditionally take the form of a play area, game room or wading pool, we found several resorts that have gone the extra mile to entertain young guests. The Disneyland Hotel, among others, offers supervised day or evening activities for kids (while moms and dads spend some time by themselves), the Konocti Harbor Inn at Clear Lake has its own miniature golf course, and the San Diego Princess rents family-sized pedal-powered carriages.

The getaways are as diverse as California families, running the gamut from back-country family camps (bring your own pillow and share a bathroom) to fancy resorts (with built-in hair dryers); small-town zoos to colossal aquariums; and snow play areas to world-class ski resorts.

Because room rates change as fast as kids' shoe sizes, specific tariffs are not included. Instead rates (per night; double occupancy) are classified this way:

Less expensive: $60 or less

Moderate: $60 to $100

Expensive: more than $100

Many hotels and motels let children stay free in their parents' room; others charge a moderate fee. Family camps, guest ranches and other resorts on the American plan (which means meals are included) generally charge a weekly, per-person rate based on age.

At the family camps, we found weekly rates (including meals and activities) ranging from a low of around $60 for a child 5 and younger, to upwards of $225 for each adult (usually age 16 or 17 and older). Privately operated guest ranches are considerably more expensive: from $200 at the low end for a young child, to $450 at the high end for an adult (per week; meals and most activities included). A call or letter to each establishment will bring a brochure and current rate information.

Using this book to do some preliminary scouting and planning, you should be able to avoid those "Children not allowed" signs. As a result of some advance work, about the only restrictions our family encounters these days are those like we found at Trinity Alps Resort, where a sign outside the children's play area forbids entry to *adults*. That's discrimination we can live with.

The Family Travel Survival Guide

Rules of the Road and Tips for Parents

1. Before leaving home, fill the kids' school-lunch boxes with travel snacks (crackers, raisins, single-serving boxes of cereal, juice and such) for the car, or even for a plane ride.

2. Let little ones pack a few of their own special things to take along.

3. Don't attempt a round trip between Eureka and San Diego on one tank. If you run out of gas, chances are that's what the family will remember most about the trip. (And they'll never let you forget it.)

4. Family outings aren't the best times for attempting endurance records of longest time between rest stops. It's a good idea to plan at least one 10-minute rest for every hour you spend in the car, even if the troops aren't begging for one. School playgrounds or city parks are good places to stop.

5. Bring along a supply of premoistened wipes (they're in the baby section of the supermarket) for the car, to wipe sticky fingers, runny noses and sweaty faces, not to the mention the messes for which they are specifically intended.

6. Consider purchasing some kind of inexpensive toy, game, activity book or craft project to occupy the kids' time while in the car. (And keep it a surprise until you're on the road.)

7. Suggest a diversion, like the alphabet game in which travelers take turns trying to spot a roadside object whose name begins with each letter of the alphabet. A variation on the same tried-and-true theme is "I'm going to grandma's house," a favorite in our own car. Players take turns choosing a different thing to take to grandma's, following the alphabet. For example, "I'm going to grandma's house and I'm taking an apple, a bear, a cauliflower," and so forth. Each player must recite the growing list on every turn.

8. Before your trip, visit the library or toy store and pick up a few cassette tapes with music or stories for your particular age group. Better yet, before the trip, record yourself reading a favorite book. (We cut deals with our kids. They get to hear one Disney story for every one of our rock-and-roll tapes.)

9. When your child gets chewing gum in his or her hair, rub some creamy peanut butter through the offending mess. If gum gets stuck on someone's clothes, put the article in a freezer. It'll chip off when frozen.

10. If you're interested in a little time alone during a vacation, take turns with your spouse (although some resorts in this book have supervised programs for kids). While one parent is jogging or shopping, the other can spend some time with the children.

11. If a family member has ear/altitude problems or motion sickness, you can receive some free tips from the American Academy of Otolaryngology. Send a self-addressed, stamped envelope to them at 1101 Vermont Avenue NW, Suite 302, Washington, D.C. 20005. By the way, watching passing scenery out the side windows from the back seat can cause queasiness. If this happens, have the young one join you in the front seat (strapped in, of course) and look straight ahead.

12. Clean, unlocked filling-station restrooms are about as common nowadays as those 1950's-era "Giant Orange" California roadside refreshment stands. Instead of stopping at a gas station where you'll likely encounter locked doors and dirty facilities, why not try a fast-food restaurant? Their restrooms are more accessible and often much cleaner.

13. Finally, be prepared for the worst. During our travels for this book, our son, healthy for the previous 12 months, became sick at Disneyland, and we ended up being transported by park security to a local hospital emergency department. If you can't be flexible when traveling with children, you're better off pitching a tent in the back yard.

Tips for Kids

1. Make sure you empty your tanks when mom and dad fill the car's tank. Parents don't appreciate potty-stop requests 10 minutes after leaving a gas station.

2. Unless you enjoy the sight of smoke coming from the driver's ears, keep the "Are we there yet?" queries to a minimum.

3. Don't tell mom or dad about that cute older guy or girl at the beach until after you get home. Being grounded during vacation is the pits.

4. Don't make fun of dad's "I ♥ Yosemite" t-shirt or mom's mouse ears—at least until the fun's over and you're back home.

I

Family Resorts and Camps, Guest Ranches and City Adventures

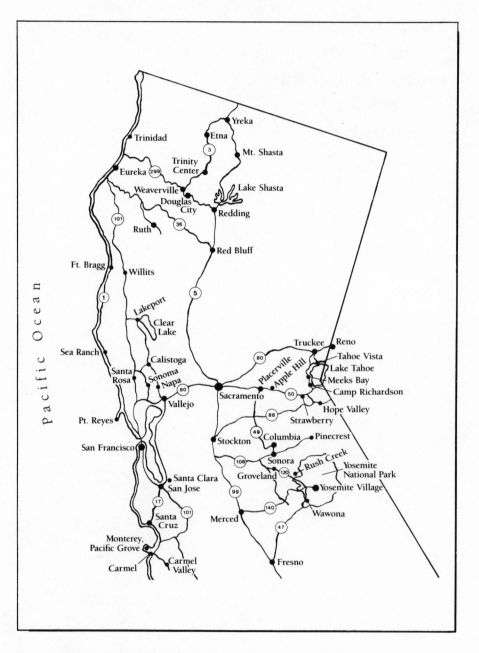

The Northern
Mountains and
Great Valley

❦

· About
Guest Ranches

❦ When I was growing up, resorts that offered
horseback riding, hay rides, campfires and chuckwagon grub were
called dude ranches. In recent years, however, the "dudes" have
pretty much gone the way of Disneyland's "E ticket." By now, most
such resorts have adopted the more genteel name of guest ranch.

Fortunately, only the name has been changed. There are no fern
bars, no trendy cuisine, no valet parking. Just lots of old-fashioned
fun and homemade food – the way it used to be.

For families seeking solace from smog, city life and school, the
remote settings of the resorts listed in this section make a visit to a
north-state guest ranch an ideal getaway. While they may be isolated,
the ranches don't scrimp on creature comforts. Most treat their
guests like family, with nicely furnished ranch-style rooms and cabins, lots of hot water, plenty of supervised activities, tennis courts
and heated pools. (Of course, you can find more amenities – or an
experience as different as a night on a paddlewheeler – in Sacramento, the last-described destination in this section of otherwise
ranch/resort destinations.)

As noted in the introduction, a week at a guest ranch isn't inexpensive. True, you'll not have much in the way of out-of-pocket expenses
up here, since meals and most activities are often included. Still, a

week for a family of four can run upwards of $1500, depending on ages. Rates do vary, however, and the resorts will gladly send you a rate sheet outlining specifics and specials. It may not be the most inexpensive vacation you'll take, but it will likely be one of the most memorable.

JH Guest Ranch

ETNA

❦ Families who want to get away from it all couldn't go much farther than the JH Guest Ranch in Etna. Where's Etna? Well, that's tough to say. It's in the Marble Mountains, just south of Greenville; a hop, skip and jump from Fort Jones, if that's any help.

Suffice it to say it's *way* up north. In fact, the proverbial crow doesn't have to fly more than 40 miles before reaching Oregon.

You'll be hard-pressed to find a more remote spot for a California family vacation. And you'll have an equally difficult time finding a more pleasant resort in all of the state. The JH Ranch is certainly worth the extra mileage.

Although we're generally skeptical of travel-brochure hype (many places look better in pictures than in person), one look at this resort's handout hooked us. The resort comprises nearly 300 acres, although there are miles and miles of more wilderness beyond the ranch boundaries.

Terrain ranges from meadowland to mountains, with lots in between. And the staff takes full advantage of their environment. Horses will take you on an easy tour of the ranch or to a remote lake on an overnighter. Or you might opt for a couple of days' worth of white-water rafting down the Klamath River (with a ranch guide).

Meanwhile, back at the ranch, guests are busy learning marksmanship on a rifle range, or playing Ping-Pong, horseshoes and shuffleboard. Hay rides are also part of the ranch itinerary.

The JH centerpiece, however, is an impressive wood and stone lodge. Inside are a western-style sitting room under pine trusses, and a sunny dining room. A solar-heated, free-form pool as well as tennis courts are nearby.

At night, folks gather at a big red barn for square dancing and talent nights.

When it's time to call it a day, guests retire to either light-housekeeping cabins that sleep four or duplex units. (Trailer and camper spaces are also available.)

During the winter, the resort doesn't shut down. It simply switches gears, offering a different set of activities like cross-country skiing and trips to the ski slopes near Ashland, Oregon. And if you've always wanted to treat the family to a white Christmas and old-fashioned yule celebration, they have that too.

Come to think of it, there aren't many activities and services that the JH Guest Ranch *doesn't* have.

JH Guest Ranch, 8525 Homestead Lane, Etna, CA 96027. Telephone (916) 467-3468. From Interstate 5 at Yreka, drive southwest on Highway 3 through Fort Jones and Etna. The resort turnoff is four miles south of Etna. Light-housekeeping cabins and duplex units, all with baths. Cribs and rollaways available. Year-round activities from swimming to skiing. American plan (meals included). Expensive.

Coffee Creek Ranch

TRINITY CENTER

❦ There are relatively few guest ranches in all of California, but visitors to tiny Trinity Center have a choice of two: the Trinity Mountain Meadow Resort and Coffee Creek Ranch.

Named for the nearby creek that flows year-round, Coffee Creek ranch sits three thousand feet up in the Trinity Alps, a dream come true for recreation enthusiasts and nirvana for those just interested in a bit of peace and quiet. The ranch offers parents and kids quite a list of things to do. I counted more than a dozen activities, including many games, archery, a rifle range, horseback riding, gold panning, hayrides, bonfires and horseshoes.

Chances are an archery lesson will not have as much appeal to your toddler as it will to you and your teenagers. But fear not. Coffee Creek offers a "Kiddie Korral" where staff members keep little ones (age 3 to 9) occupied with fun and games while you indulge in your own fun and games.

Don't worry about having to fight the crowds during a visit to Coffee Creek. Because most folks come up here to enjoy some solitude, the ranch limits its guest list to 60 each week. Families stay in secluded two-bedroom cabins (two have fireplaces) or ranch-house rooms overlooking the pool. Rooms are available on a per-night basis during winter, as well as during the summer as space permits.

Although the resort provides many comforts of home, marking the passage of time isn't important up here. If you want to wake up at a certain hour, remember this is strictly a B.Y.O.C. resort. (That's "bring your own clock.")

Coffee Creek Ranch, Star Route 2, Box 4940, Trinity Center, CA 96091. Telephone (916) 266-3343. From Redding, take Highway 299 past Whiskeytown Lake. Take Lewiston Lake/Trinity Dam turnoff to Highway 3. Drive north past Trinity Center to Coffee Creek Road. Turn left to resort. Fourteen cabins and ranch house rooms, all with baths. Cribs and rollaways available. Generally open April through December. Numerous activities, including tennis and swimming pool. American plan (meals included). Expensive.

Trinity Mountain Meadow Resort

TRINITY CENTER

❦ An Alpine meadow surrounded by majestic snow-capped peaks provides an awesome setting for Trinity Mountain Meadow Resort. This tidy resort is one of two guest ranches hidden away along this portion of California's "Alps."

The Mountain Meadow Resort couldn't be better oriented to the care and feeding of families. In fact, other California resorts could learn a thing or two from the folks who run this show.

Sure, they offer the requisite guest-ranch diversions: horseback riding, hiking, swimming, volleyball and badminton. But the resort also has a foot-deep wading pool to separate the tots from teens, different activities for the varying age groups represented each week (crafts, hikes, drama), and daytime child care. We were likewise impressed by a somewhat unusual service. Because many children often seem to get hungry for dinner before adults (especially if they've been running hither and yon all day), the resort serves dinner in two shifts. An early dinner hour for kids supervised by staff members precedes the later adult meal. More organized activities for kids get under way when mom and dad sit down to their supper.

Traveling twosomes are quartered in the smaller upstairs lodge rooms while families are assigned nearby cabins, each with its own bath. The cabins hold up to six people.

Although the upstairs rooms do have pretty views, there are so many outdoor activities to enjoy that you'll not likely have the time – or inclination – to sit indoors and stare out the window.

Trinity Mountain Meadow Resort, 24225 Summit Woods Drive, Los Gatos, CA 95030 (October to May address); or Star Route 2, Box 5700, Trinity Center, CA 96091 (June to September address). Telephone (408) 353-1663 (winter) or (916) Fort Jones Operator, Sawyers Bar 4677 (summer). Generally open June through August. From Redding (two-and-a-half hours), take Highway 299 past Whiskeytown Lake. Take the Lewiston Lake/Trinity Dam turnoff to Highway 3, then drive north to Coffee Creek Road. The resort is 18 miles up the road. Ten cabins with private bath. Cribs and rollaways available. American plan (meals included). Expensive.

Trinity Alps Resort

TRINITY LAKE

✿ Ever since the 1920's, city folks have looked to the Trinity Alps Resort for what the management promises as "the rest of your life." And when we dropped by one spring day, there was some serious loafing going on.

Most of it was happening in and around the 40 vintage wooden cabins that hug both sides of a gorgeous stretch of the Stuart Fork River. (A suspension foot bridge serves as a thoroughfare over the river.) The comfy old cabins, named after California counties, are nestled among the pines and come with rear sleeping verandas that beg for midday snoozing as well as overnighters under the stars.

At this full-service resort above Weaverville, there's either nothing to do or a lot to do. The best part is, *you* get to decide how much or how little. If your intention is to do nothing, the folks here make it easy. There's fresh air, lots of places to sit and think about it and no phones, TVs or schedules.

Rustic family cabins are tucked close to the Stuart Fork River at Trinity Alps Resort.

If you're otherwise inclined, plenty of activities are offered to keep you and/or the kids entertained. The tree-fringed tennis courts were busy during our visit, as was a river swimming hole. There's also volleyball, badminton and horseshoes. Younger kids enjoyed "Fort Trinity," a special play area containing climbing structures and other equipment. The resort operates a camp store, pool hall and game room, soda fountain and fellowship hall.

Organized activities include square dancing, trail rides (including breakfast rides), bingo, movies, bonfires and sing-alongs.

While the homey resort's family-style dining hall bustles three times a day, many guests prepare meals (and save a few dollars) in their cabins. Each has a barbeque and kitchen with stove, icebox, pots, pans, dishes and utensils.

Reservations at the resort are booked for week-long stays (Saturday through Saturday). Some families make a party of it and bring along friends, since the two-bedroom cabins can sleep up to 10. (There are also one-bedroom units that accommodate up to 4.)

Guests can either tote up their own linen or pay an extra fee for a week's worth of bedding.

In terms of a mountain experience, the Trinity Alps Resort gets a four-star rating from our family. My old Boy Scout leaders would be ashamed, but we're not a camping family–in the down-and-dirty sense of the term. We'd rather not squeeze into a tent, use a latrine, share restrooms for a week with dozens of strangers or eat powdered eggs over a campfire day after day.

We enjoy niceties like (private) hot showers, real beds, electricity, a wooden floor and a choice between cooking or "dining out."

But at the same time, we treasure rustic surroundings, clean air, the sound of a river nearby and the smell of the woods. An impossible dream? Anyone who scoffs hasn't been up here.

Trinity Alps Resort, Star Route, Box 490, Lewiston, CA 96052. Telephone (916) 286-2205. From Weaverville, drive 14 miles north on Highway 3. Turn left on Trinity Alps Road and drive 1 mile to the resort. Generally open Memorial Day through Labor Day. Forty rustic cabins, all with electricity, baths, furnished kitchens and sleeping verandas. Cribs and rollaways available. Swimming beach, horseback riding, tennis, volleyball, badminton, Ping-Pong, children's play area, movies, square dancing and bingo. On-site family restaurant, store and Christian fellowship hall. European plan (meals not included). Available on weekly basis. Inexpensive to moderate.

Indian Creek Lodge

DOUGLAS CITY

❦ When planning a visit to the Trinity County area, figure on spending at least a couple of nights. That is, unless you live in Redding, Red Bluff or some other nearby north-state community. You'll need at least a day or two to unwind after the long drive from central- or south-state cities.

If your destination isn't one of the region's full-service guest ranches or a wooded campground, Indian Creek Lodge is a good choice for a place to call home during a visit.

We found the lodge to be one of the nicer facilities in the area. Four acres of lawn give guests plenty of space to spread out, and the swing set was a welcome sight for our youngsters, who had been cooped up in the car for hours.

Behind the lodge, the grass sweeps down to the Trinity River, which provides good swimming and innertubing possibilities during the summer.

The lodge's smaller rooms, while comfortable, were nothing to write home about. However, the suites are spacious and, in our opinion, probably worth the extra $10 or so per day. Some have river-view decks, kitchens and barbeques.

While morning brings the smell of clean mountain air, evenings here are invariably filled with the aroma of a fresh catch-of-the-day being grilled by the fisherman occupying the room next door. A good reason to get acquainted with the neighbors.

Indian Creek Lodge, P.O. Box 100, Douglas City, CA 96024. Telephone (916) 623-6294. From Redding, drive west on Highway 299 for 35 miles to the lodge. The lodge is 9 miles south of Weaverville, near the Highway 3/299 junction. Fourteen rooms, five with kitchens, and all with private baths and TV. Kitchen units have decks and barbeques. Cribs and rollaways available. Inexpensive to moderate.

Diversions

The Trinity Alps, a fishermen's paradise since the early days, are rich in other forms of recreation as well. Whiskeytown Lake, about a half-hour from the lodge, has some 150 miles of shoreline. It's a popular destination for water skiers and swimmers. Beautiful Trinity Lake, too, is nearby. Visitors should allow time to visit Weaverville and the town's museum, stamp mill (a working replica) and Chinese Joss House Historical Landmark.

Flying Double A Ranch

RUTH

❧ Experiencing a California guest ranch doesn't necessarily require a big investment of time and money. Most ranch resorts in these parts ask visitors to spend at least several days, but the Flying Double A is set up for overnight stays as well as more extended visits.

The Flying Double A offers many of the activities you'll find at its north-state cousins. Here you'll have access to horseback riding, swimming in a heated pool, tennis (two courts), fishing, hay rides, trap shooting, barbeques and even bike rentals for exploring the area. The ranch recreation room contains table and video games and a stage for special shows. And because the Flying Double A is a working cattle ranch, you're often able to watch cowboys practicing their craft outside your door.

Accommodations here range from motel-type rooms and family units to tents. Our family of four spent a spring night in two deck-top tents, the boys in one, the girls in the other. Each tent has a table, lamp, beds and portable heater.

From the deck of the lodge, visitors have a view of South Fork Mountain, the longest in the continental U.S. Ruth Lake is eight miles away, and Mad River is a less-than-half-mile hike.

The wide open space of Trinity County is also visible from the ranch restaurant, an informal cafe where friendly staff serve up hearty portions of good food. Occasionally, approaching pilots (there's a small airport on-site) can be heard over the radio in the restaurant asking a waitress about weather conditions or ordering dinner – in advance.

The Flying Double A isn't the easiest resort to get to. On your California map, trace the path of Highway 36 west from Interstate 5 at Red Bluff. The ranch, accessible by plane or by tortuous Highway 36, is situated near Ruth about midway between Interstate 5 and Highway 101.

We were told the trip from Eureka is easier than the route we took out of Red Bluff. However, the night we stayed here, planes outnumbered cars. That's about as far off the beaten path as you can get.

Flying Double A Ranch, Ruth Star Route, Box 700, Bridgeville, CA

Swimming in a heated pool high in the Trinity Alps is a favorite summer pastime at Flying Double A Ranch.

95526. Telephone (707) 574-6227. From Highway 36 near Bridgeville, Trinity County, follow signs south to Ruth. The resort is 22 miles from Highway 36 (112 miles from Red Bluff). Forty-eight rooms (and tents), half with private baths. Cribs and rollaways available. Swimming, tennis, trap shooting and bike rentals. Restaurant on-site. Generally open April through Labor Day. Less expensive to expensive.

Emandal:
A Farm on a River
WILLITS

❧ Admitting it would have been less than cool, but my city friends and I secretly envied our peers who grew up in the country.

Taking out the garbage and mowing the lawn were drudgery. What we longed for was a real live "chore": gathering eggs, milking a cow or feeding the chickens. I'm certain the country kids complained as loudly as we did, but life on a farm has always held a certain mystique.

For city parents interested in giving their kids a taste of country life – without moving – Emandal might be just the ticket. Around the turn of the century, the owners of this "farm on a river" began opening the property to friends from the Bay Area. Although the farm changed hands in the 1940's, the tradition continues. Each summer, beginning in late July, the welcome mat comes out and families start rolling in. Most stay for a week (or longer), although cabins, when available, can be rented for shorter stays.

The pace at Emandal is slow. The owners have intentionally created a low-pressure atmosphere, believing that visiting families "need time to be together in an unstructured environment."

The absence of planned activities notwithstanding, visitors keep busy sampling the region's natural beauty and recreational opportunities. For example, the scenic Eel River flows along three miles of Emandal, creating great summer swimming spots.

Back on the farm, lots of diversions lend themselves to family enjoyment. Although farm chores (like gathering eggs) are perennial, many activities change with the calendar. During the farm's "seasonal country weekends," there are garden planting (in the spring), harvesting and apple pressing (in the fall) and wreath making (in winter).

Nineteen redwood cabins built among the trees back in the 1920's still provide shelter for Emandal visitors. (Bath and shower facilities are located in an adjacent area.) Each cabin has beds, cold spring water and electricity. And you won't have to look farther than the nearest tree for a hammock.

Emandal, 16500 Hearst Post Office Road, Willits, CA 95490. Telephone (707) 459-5439. Sixteen miles east of Willits and Highway 101. Contact farm for detailed map. Nineteen rustic cabins with electricity and cold water. Bath facilities are separate. Week-long stays are encouraged; shorter stays allowed when space is available. American plan (meals included). Expensive.

Diversions

The popular California Western Railroad "Skunk" trains, which used to haul lumber, now carry tourists on regular scenic runs through 40 miles of hills and redwood forest between Willits and Fort Bragg. The round trip takes eight-and-a-half hours. (Plan on spending at least $50 for a family of three. Kids under five ride free on mom's or dad's lap.) A shorter, four-hour excursion between Willits and Northspur is also offered.

Greenhorn Creek
Guest Ranch

QUINCY

❦ Greenhorn Creek Guest Ranch sits in the midst of the big-tree country of California's northern Sierra: land of a hundred lakes and a thousand miles of mountain streams; a horseman's paradise and photographer's dream.

The casinos of Lake Tahoe and Reno are only about an hour's drive south, but I'll wager you'll not get the gambling urge or have any desire to set foot in the car during your stay here. There's simply too much to do—or not to do, depending on your frame of mind.

The proprietors call this place "Shangri-La of Feather River Country," which may just be an understatement. A million acres of national forest surround you, a nightly "rainbow ballet" of jumping fish serenade you, and, possibly best of all, someone else does the cooking. It doesn't get much better than this.

While a week at Greenhorn Creek will certainly bring you closer to your family, it also offers kids and parents an opportunity to pursue some independent activities. During the day, adults can leave the children in the trustworthy hands of the resident "female wrangler" for swimming, fishing, ponyback riding and other supervised activities. Mom and dad are free to fish, ride, hike, golf, explore or snooze in hammocks.

When the sun sets, the fish in the ranch pond aren't the only ones who begin to jump and dance. Evenings at Greenhorn Creek mean square dancing. And don't try to bow out with the excuse that you don't know how to swing "yer pardner." There are free group lessons.

Other evening diversions here include frog racing, rope spinning,

"Greenies" cross a river the old-fashioned way at Greenhorn Creek Guest Ranch.

guest amateur night and a bonfire complete with storytelling, singing and plenty of marshmallows and homemade cake and ice cream.

Greenhorn Creek Guest Ranch, Spring Garden P.O. Box 7010-FG, Quincy, CA 95971-7010. Telephone (916) 283-0930. Off Highway 70/89 about 65 miles north of Lake Tahoe, 10 miles south of Quincy. Open March through November. Modern western-style accommodations. Included in weekly rates (daily stays are available if space permits) are room, meals, horseback riding, trout fishing, swimming and other activities. Free instruction in horseback riding, rope spinning and square dancing. Expensive.

Bridge Bay Resort

LAKE SHASTA

❦ If your family is looking for some Shasta action, this patriarch of lakeside resorts is *the* spot. Situated at Shasta's southern central end, 12 minutes north of Redding and a stone's throw from Interstate 5, Bridge Bay Resort is one of the lake's most conveniently located destinations. And with 40 rooms and an impressive armada of rental boats, it's certainly among the best equipped.

A favorite among boating families, Bridge Bay Resort has about as much presence on the water as off. A sprawling set of floating garages stretches out into the lake and an adjacent pier is usually crammed with rental houseboats.

The multiwinged motel is set against a lush hillside overlooking the lake. Barbeques and picnic tables sit in front of several of the rooms. Many have lake views.

Accommodations range from rooms with two double beds to kitchen suites that sleep up to eight. A pool overlooks the lake.

If you're among the minority who arrive without a boat and a serious case of boat envy sets in, the resort will rent you one. Fishing boats, patio boats and ski boats are all available for as little as four hours or as long as a week or more. (Daily rates run between about $50 for a fishing boat to about $200 for a family patio boat.) Guests who bring their own boats don't pay a launch fee. "Land lubber" package deals are offered at the resort during the off-season (September through May).

Bridge Bay Resort, 10300 Bridge Bay Road, Redding, CA 96003. Telephone (916) 275-3021. From Interstate 5, 12 miles north of Redding, take the Bridge Bay exit to the resort. Forty rooms and suites, some with kitchens. Pool, lake access, launching and moorage, boat rentals, store, restaurant and snack bar. Inexpensive to moderate.

Sugarloaf Cottages Resort

LAKE SHASTA

❦ Despite its three-hundred-plus miles of shoreline, Lake Shasta is, by California resort-area standards, remarkably undeveloped. It's a mixed blessing. Pleasure boaters and fishermen glide along the shore for miles and miles without seeing any hint of civilization. But if you're looking for a nice family resort, the pickings are slim.

We found one at Lakehead, a mile or so off Interstate 5 below Lakeshore Drive. A cluster of small, modern cabins and townhouse units, Sugarloaf Cottages Resort occupies a shady spot just steps from the Sacramento River arm of the big lake.

For access to Shasta's warm waters (summer water temperatures average 72 degrees), Sugarloaf is hard to beat. There's a private dock for sunbathing, swimming, fishing or launching the family boat. And when the troops aren't occupied with water sports, there are badminton, horseshoes, volleyball, Ping-Pong and kids' play equipment available on the grounds.

With only 15 units, Sugarloaf is relatively small, so you'll be sharing the resort with few other folks. And because rooms go for week-long minimums during the summer (daily rates are offered September to May), long vacations here will give you a chance to get to know the neighbors in the cabin next door.

The one-, two- and three-bedroom units are tastefully decorated and feature air conditioning, pine panelling and fully equipped kitchens with microwave ovens. Sleeping capacity ranges up to 12 people.

Sugarloaf Cottages Resort, Star Route, Box 845, Lakeshore Drive, Lakehead, CA 96051. Telephone (916) 238-2448. From northbound Interstate 5, take the Lakeshore Drive exit and turn left. The resort is three miles down the road on the left. Fifteen contemporary cottages and townhouses, most with lake views. All have kitchens, air conditioning and barbeques. Play equipment, games, private dock; boat slip included. Minimum one-week stay during summer. Restaurant on-site. Summer: expensive. Off-season: moderate to expensive.

Sacramento

🐭 Like thousands of Northern California kids, my first impressions of Sacramento were formed during a field trip back in elementary school. While my tour of the capitol and Sutter's Fort were memorable, nothing much else about the city made an impression. How things have changed!

No longer a town where politics and agriculture rule, Sacramento is forging a new image built on rich historic roots and plentiful outdoor recreation, as well as ambitious growth. Sacramento's appeal isn't much of a secret anymore. More than 11 million people are dropping by every year. California's capital is now the sixth-largest city in the state. Following are some suggestions for your itinerary.

Old Sacramento

The Gold Rush established Sacramento as "gateway to the Mother Lode," and much of the city's historic section has been recreated or preserved, down to the cobblestone streets and plank sidewalks. Now a state historic park, the area between Interstate 5 and the Sacramento River (known now as Old Sacramento) is considered one of the nation's best examples of historic reconstruction.

In addition to classic Western-style old buildings, many of which house museum exhibits, there are plenty of candy and knick-knack shops, a one-room school with vintage play equipment, horse-drawn carriages, riverboat rides and short excursions aboard a steam-powered passenger train.

The State Capitol

A walk through the newly restored state capitol (10th Street and Capitol Mall) is enough to make even the most stingy taxpayer proud. During an extensive project that lasted several years, workers returned the grand old building to its turn-of-the-century appearance. Kids of all ages seem to enjoy the free informative tours. (Treks up and down the flights of stairs allowed the young ones on our tour to blow off some steam.) Of particular interest are the first-floor re-creations of offices as they appeared long ago.

The Delta King, *sister ship of the famous* Delta Queen, *plied inland waterways before being restored along the Old Sacramento waterfront.*

California State Railroad Museum

Definitely in a class all its own hereabouts, the State Railroad Museum in Old Sacramento is perhaps the finest of its kind in the world. From a child's point of view, there's nothing else like it in the entire state. You can climb aboard an old mail car, gaze at the gleaming *Governor Stanford* steam locomotive and stroll through a vintage sleeping-car exhibit that shakes as if it's rolling down the rails. Many of the nearly two dozen restored locomotives and train cars are set in interpretive exhibits. Be sure to begin your tour here by watching the short movie in the museum theater. The real-life scene that reveals itself after the film will knock your socks off.

William Land Park

There are three main attractions in expansive municipal William Land Park: Fairytale Town, the amusement center and the Sacramento Zoo. Fairytale Town is a six-acre playground whose "sets" are based on well-known fairy tales. The adjacent amusement center offers midway-type rides on a small scale.

Although San Diego's and San Francisco's respective zoos get the, er, lion's share of attention in California, Sacramento's own zoo is one of the best. In fact, several visitors we talked to ranked the Sacramento facility tops in Northern California. While San Franciscans will scoff at such a comparison, Sacramento's collection of animals, habitats and zoo grounds is impressive. The reptile house is always chock full of exotic creatures, including a Gila monster and about a hundred snakes.

There's also a flamingo exhibit, a hoofed-animal complex, a great-ape habitat and several hundred other animals, among them elephants, giraffes and a hippo, as well as numerous felines. (Take Interstate 5 south from Sacramento to Sutterville Road.)

Sutter's Fort

A popular Sacramento tourist stop since it became part of the state park system in the 1940's, Sutter's Fort is a reconstructed version of John Sutter's Gold Rush–era adobe settlement.

Upon entering the fort, visitors are given personal listening devices that activate recorded narratives at each exhibit. A bakery, weaving room, blacksmith's shop, bunk room, Sutter's original office complex and other exhibits typify life in Sacramento during the 1840's.

Outside the walls of the fort is the State Indian Museum (27th and L streets). Other Sacramento points of interest include the new Towe Museum of antique Ford autos (at 2200 Front Street), Waterworld USA (see Water Parks section in Part III of this book), Nimbus Fish Hatchery (near the Hazel Avenue Bridge over the American River off Highway 50), the California State Fair (in summer) and Gibson Ranch County Park (take Watt Avenue north to Elverta Road). The small Folsom Zoo (in nearby Folsom) is a kind of foster home for exotic animals that were once ill-gotten private pets and for other creatures with injuries that prevent them from living in the wilds (like a lion with failing kidneys and a blind eagle).

Spending the Night?

You don't have to travel cross-country to sleep on a genuine riverboat. The *Delta King*, whose sister ship the *Delta Queen* now plies the Mississippi, was rescued from years of neglect and is permanently berthed on the river at Old Sacramento. The restored paddlewheeler is now a floating hotel.

The North Coast

❦

Sea Ranch

SONOMA COUNTY

❦ If your image of a vacation at the seashore includes lots of swimming, sun and tanning lotion, you'll generally have the best luck south of San Francisco. On the other hand, if you'd prefer an uncrowded getaway along some of California's most dramatic coastline, the Sea Ranch is the place.

Visitors here have a couple of accommodation options, each offering a different experience. The Sea Ranch Lodge offers a set of comfortable rooms, all of which have ocean views. Some have fireplaces and private hot tubs. (There are no telephones or TVs.) There's also a restaurant here, as well as a small store.

Perched on a bluff overlooking the ocean, the lodge is only part of the "ranch." Mostly it comprises privately owned coastal vacation homes, many of which can be rented.

One rental agency sent us a listing of dozens of available homes along with detailed descriptions of each, including those that do not welcome children. (There are many with no restrictions.)

All the homes are nicely furnished (including the kitchens), although guests must bring their own linens and towels.

Two-night rental rates ranged from about $150 to more than $300. Weekly rates are also offered. None allows more than eight people.

Guests have access to the North Recreation Center, which contains an Olympic-size pool, three tennis courts, saunas and basketball and volleyball courts. The golf course here is rated among the top 10 in California. Young children will enjoy the swings and slides. Stable facilities are in the planning stage. The "hot spot" is a beach on the Gualala River offering swimming behind a seasonal dam in a forested setting. Ocean beaches are accessible via stairways and trails.

With crumbling bluffs, rocky points and beaches that become inundated rapidly at high tide, Sea Ranch is not a place where small children should have free run. (Some homes are set along bluff areas that could be dangerous to little ones. The rental agencies will help you select just the right place.) But with the proper dose of parental supervision, it's definitely one of the north coast's best bets for an enjoyable family getaway.

Sea Ranch Lodge, P.O. Box 44, Sea Ranch, CA 95497. Telephone (707) 785-2371. The resort is 110 miles north of San Francisco on Highway 1 in Sonoma County. Ocean-view rooms and suites, some with fireplaces and hot tubs. Cribs and rollaways available. Restaurant and golf course. Expensive.

Sea Ranch homes, located north of Sea Ranch Lodge on either side of Highway 101. Furnished vacation homes, all with kitchens and fireplaces, some with hot tubs and other amenities. Guests have privileges at rec center with pool, tennis, basketball and saunas. Resort also has children's play area, golf course, river swimming beach and ocean beaches. Rental agencies include Beach Rentals, (707) 884-4005; Rams Head Realty, (707) 785-2427; and Sea Ranch Rentals, (707) 785-2579. Moderate to expensive.

Eureka

❦ Families who enjoy the California seashore but not the seemingly ever-present crowds are facing a dilemma these days. With the increasing hordes of people that descend on most coastal resort communities during vacation season, the choice between the backyard patio and the beach is getting more difficult.

For a growing number of travelers-in-the-know, however, Humboldt County—Eureka in particular—is emerging as an uncrowded, albeit cool and sometimes damp, coastal getaway alternative. With the exception of generous amounts of sunshine that bless the central and south coast much of the year, Eureka has just about all the ingredients for a fun family adventure.

The county's average temperature is just a shade below 58 degrees. True, it's a lot warmer in San Diego or even Santa Cruz. But a chilly morning up here can be invigorating. And when the sun does occasionally dare reveal itself, this region is nothing short of glorious.

If you're driving up from the south (there's not much more California to the north), take your time getting into town. There's plenty to see in the southern part of the county. Many take the scenic route along the 33-mile-long Avenue of the Giants. Keep in mind that this historic stretch of old Highway 101, which winds along the Eel River, will add about an hour to your drive. It's an hour well spent, however.

These coast redwoods are the tallest living trees in the world, often reaching 300 feet into the sky. The earth's tallest tree, all 368 feet of it, sinks its roots here. The kids will likely pester you for a photo of them inside the drive-through tree at Myers Flat.

Plan on spending at least a day touring Eureka. Old Town (along the waterfront) has been renovated and revitalized and now holds lots of intriguing shops and eateries.

Sequoia Park and Zoo (Glatt and W streets) sits at the edge of a redwood grove. The children's playground, zoo and (in the summer) petting zoo are gathering places for local and visiting families alike.

There aren't too many old forts around California, but there's one here that's open to the public. Fort Humboldt, now a state historic park, served as Gen. U. S. Grant's headquarters for a time. There's a historic logging display here, as well as other "neat old stuff."

You can view the city from the water by hopping aboard a Humboldt Bay cruise ship at the foot of C Street. Special rates for kids make this an inexpensive as well as enjoyable 75 minutes.

If rain keeps you from enjoying the outdoors, there are a few museums scattered about the county: the Hoopa Tribal Museum in Hoopa, Fortuna Depot Museum in Fortuna, Clarke Memorial Museum in Eureka and the Pacific Lumber Company Museum in nearby Scotia.

Scores of beautiful Victorians make Eureka an architectural museum itself. The Chamber of Commerce will supply you with a "drive-by tour" map showing locations of more than a hundred grand old residences. All you supply are the wheels. Just make sure the windshield wipers are in good working order.

Looking as if it was created by the Brothers Grimm, Eureka's gingerbread Carson Mansion inspires "oohs" from even the most weary travelers.

Spending the Night?

The Eureka Inn, (707) 442-6441, is a Tudor-style landmark, in operation since the 1920's. It has been nicely restored, and has a pool and spa. Moderate to expensive.

The Eagle House B&B Inn, (707) 442-2334, is a remodeled Victorian Hotel situated in Old Town. Moderate to expensive.

The Best Western Thunderbird Lodge, (800) 528-1234; Carson House Inn, (707) 443-1601; and Red Lion Motor Inn, (707) 445-0844, all have comfortable rooms, swimming pools and spas.

Bishop Pine Lodge
TRINIDAD

🐝 If he enjoys combing the beach but she'd rather hike through the forest, don't give up. It's a bit of a drive for southlanders – and even central Californians – but Bishop Pine Lodge is a tree-and-sea resort that manages to combine the best of California.

The lodge consists of a baker's dozen secluded cabins surrounded by gardens and redwoods. The well-kept, yellow-shuttered cottages all have showers, and most have tiny kitchens tucked into corner nooks. There are three two-bedroom units for larger groups.

Although the cabins have television and cable movie channels, even the most diehard couch potatoes will be tempted by the outdoor environment here. Several hiking trails begin on the grounds, meandering through the north coastal forest area. (Bring a basket during berry season.) For younger visitors, a playground is set up at the lodge.

It's only a few hundred yards to the seashore, a favorite among driftwood collectors, clam hunters and rock hounds. One of California's least-known state parks – Patrick's Point – covers more than four hundred acres of forest and meadowland here.

At Agate Beach, chances are you'll see more fannies than faces. No, this isn't a nude beach. These bodies are clothed. It's just that the natural treasures spread over the sand are too much to resist for beachcombers. Most folks spend their time here hunched over combing through the small rocks and shells that are constantly thrown onto the beach by wave action. It's an activity that looks comical from a distance, but you'll be hard-pressed to resist.

One thing you won't find at the lodge is a pool. The cool weather up here makes such amenities impractical, although there is a safe swimming beach at Big Lagoon County Park if the weather's cooperative.

Bishop Pine Lodge, 1481 Patrick's Point Drive, Trinidad, CA 95570.

Telephone (707) 677-3314. From northbound Highway 101, take the Trinidad exit and drive north on Patrick's Point Drive (old 101) for two miles. Thirteen one- and two-bedroom cottages, all with private baths. Ten with kitchen facilities. Cribs and rollaways available. Moderate.

The Wine
Country

🍇

Konocti Harbor Inn

KELSEYVILLE
(CLEAR LAKE)

🍇 The marvelous resorts of Yosemite, Lake Tahoe
and the coast notwithstanding, I'm inclined to bestow the honor of
Northern California's best all-around family resort on Konocti Harbor Inn.

We had been hearing glowing reports about this destination for
many years, but it wasn't until I began searching out family getaways
that we finally made the trek to Clear Lake.

Unless you're a boating enthusiast (none of us is), there's not
much else to attract your family to Clear Lake. As California's largest
natural lake, the region certainly has potential, but we found many
of the lake's accommodations uninspired and disappointing. Then
we arrived at the Konocti.

Our first impressions were formed at the resort security gate,
where the uniformed guard gave us an indication that the Konocti
cares about who's coming in. (It's a concern shared by any responsi-
ble parent.)

The twisting drive down to the lakeshore offers a panoramic view
of the lush complex and water. Many of the two-story motel-type
wings of the resort are on terraces of the hill, providing most guests
with blue-water views. The 250 rooms and suites are air conditioned

and nicely appointed. There are also apartments and cottages on the grounds. Some have kitchens.

This isn't the type of place that lends itself to spending lots of time in your room, however. In terms of family activities and facilities, you name it and the Konocti's likely got it.

While the lake is a huge swimming hole in itself, the Konocti sports two lake-view Olympic-size pools as well as two wading pools for little folk. Next to the pool area is a children's play area that would rival a well-equipped school playground. These facilities sit at the edge of the lake near the marina and lodge.

A short walk up the manicured hillside past the motel units and over a footbridge is another recreation area, with a challenging miniature golf course presided over by hulking dinosaurs, ghosts and kangaroos. Next door is a spacious recreation center with pool tables and video games.

Supervised activities are offered for youngsters during both day and evening hours. Movies, dances and bingo are popular for visiting children. There are also eight lighted tennis courts. Four golf courses are located nearby.

In addition, the Konocti offers various options for enjoying Clear Lake. If you bring a boat, you can use the launch facilities here. The resort also rents boats and water skis, and maintains its own paddle-wheel excursion vessel for sightseeing cruises.

According to Native American lore, a chieftain named Konocti battled here with a rival leader who fancied Konocti's daughter Lupiyoma. In the ensuing battle, both men were killed. Clear Lake, as the story goes, was created by the tears of the distraught maiden.

Konocti Harbor Inn, 8727 Soda Bay Road, Kelseyville, CA 95451 (Clear Lake). Telephone (707) 279-4281 or, toll-free in California, (800) 862-4930. The resort is five miles off Soda Bay Road along the southwestern shore of Clear Lake, about two-and-a-half hours north of San Francisco. Two hundred fifty rooms, suites and apartments, all with private baths, some with kitchens and lake views. Four swimming and wading pools, eight tennis courts, golf courses nearby, miniature golf course on-site, recreation center, supervised youth activities, restaurant, lounge and marina with boat rentals and launch facilities. Moderate to expensive.

Mountain Home
Ranch

CALISTOGA

🐝 With dozens of chic hotels and quaint bed-and-breakfast inns, there's virtually no limit to accommodations in Northern California's wine country–for adults, that is. The choices begin to narrow when you bring the whole family. While some of the trendy inns will "accept" you and your children, chances are the resident newlyweds won't appreciate the pitter-patter of little feet and giggling up and down the hall.

At Mountain Home Ranch, on the other hand, taking care of families has been a time-honored tradition for four generations. "We do not have manicured lawns or luxury rooms," notes the ranch brochure. "But the accommodations are large and comfortable."

The accommodations referred to consist of "all-weather" cabins, rustic, no-frills cabins and rooms in the ranch's main lodge. The all-weather units have multiple beds and decks or porches and come with bedding. In the rustic cabins, you bring your own bedding and towels.

We dropped by the ranch during the winter and, there being no one in the office, we showed ourselves around the grounds, accompanied by a resident dog.

The ranch is open most of the year. From February to June and September to December, lodging is on the European plan (meals, except for continental breakfast, not included). On Memorial Day weekend and from mid-June to early September, the American plan (meals included) is in effect. Meals are served family style in the dining room inside the main building.

Nestled among the hills above quaint Calistoga, Mountain Home Ranch is a good home base for families interested in poking around the wine country. The ranch also offers its own diversions, including a swimming pool (the summers can be blistering up here), tennis court and a small lake for fishing.

Mountain Home Ranch, Calistoga, CA 94515. Telephone (707) 942-6616. From Calistoga, drive north one mile to Petrified Forest Road; turn left and drive two-and-a-half miles to Mountain Home Ranch Road. Turn right and drive to ranch. Eighteen modern and rustic cabins. Rollaways available. Pool, tennis court, restaurant (summer only) and store. American plan (meals included: summer) and European plan (winter). Moderate to expensive.

Diversions

The Old Faithful Geyser (of California, that is) is a mile north of Calistoga on Tubbs Lane off Highway 29. The Petrified Forest is also nearby. There are playgrounds at Pioneer Park in Calistoga, Crane Park in St. Helena and at Yountville City Park. The Calistoga Area Park Commission maintains lighted tennis courts and indoor and outdoor racquetball courts. A hiking trail in Robert Louis Stevenson Park north of Calistoga leads to the top of Mount St. Helena.

The
San Francisco
Bay Area

❦

The Marin Coast

❦ Despite its reputation as a haven for hot-tub-bound yuppies, Marin ranks high on the list of California counties offering the greatest family getaway potential.

The northwestern coastal area of Marin, which holds much of the county's beauty, was set aside in the mid-1960's by President Kennedy as the Pacific coast's first "national seashore." The hundred-square-mile Point Reyes National Seashore holds a veritable trove of natural treasures.

They say more than two million visitors a year visit this area. I'm convinced about half of them drop by to watch the whales swim lazily by Point Reyes Lighthouse. Several years ago, we drove right to the lighthouse parking lot and enjoyed an uncrowded visual feast of passing whales. Recently, however, we had to literally take a number and wait for an hour at a nearby beach before the rangers allowed us onto the lighthouse road. It's well worth the wait, however. Our kids, who have a difficult time scanning the horizon for whale spurts from a beach, had no trouble at all spying a few from the lighthouse, three hundred feet above the water. Kids also seem to enjoy navigating the more than four hundred steps down to the lighthouse.

Not all of the region is as foggy and windy as the Point Reyes Lighthouse is much of the year. At Tomales Bay State Park, you'll find swimmers enjoying Hearts Desire Beach through October and November, when the water temperature can be as warm as 80 degrees. (Lifeguards are on duty during the summer.) Another popular swimming area is Stinson Beach, south of Bolinas.

Among Marin County's many other points of interest are the Miwok Indian Village replica at Point Reyes National Seashore, the redwoods of Muir Woods National Monument (with self-guided marked paths) and the quaint little towns of Sausalito and Tiburon.

One of Sausalito's best-kept secrets is the sprawling Bay-Delta Model, a warehouse-size research model of the San Francisco Bay and San Joaquin delta areas. Hydraulic pumps move water through an intricate series of channels and rivers, simulating tidal activity. Most visitors—even little ones—are amazed at the complexity of the waterways that this region comprises.

Angel Island, also part of Marin County, is accessible by ferry from Tiburon or San Francisco. The island, whose principal inhabitants are deer, has hiking and bike trails, picnic areas and historic buildings.

Spending the Night?

The Corte Madera Inn, just off Highway 101 in Corte Madera, is about 10 minutes north of San Francisco. In addition to comfortable rooms, the inn offers a children's play area, two spas, large outdoor pool, wading pool and fitness equipment.

San Francisco

❦ Where do you take the family when visiting San Francisco? Ask a dozen parents and you'll probably get as many, varying answers.

Over the course of our two generations' worth of excursions to the city-by-the-bay, we've visited many places. (Some, like Playland-by-the-Beach, are gone.) But we usually find ourselves drawn to the same tried-and-true adventures we experienced as kids. Following are a few favorites.

Golden Gate Park

This sprawling park is a good place to start your San Francisco family outing. We hesitated for a moment before venturing into the California Academy of Sciences with a five-year-old, fearing the onset of "museum syndrome," whose symptoms, well known to parents, include sudden fatigue, whining and boredom. As it turned out, our daughter was enthralled with each of the academy's facilities – particularly the Steinhart Aquarium and Natural History Museum.

At the aquarium, visitors can handle sea creatures in the "touching tidepool" and become dizzy watching an array of sea life zoom around a 360-degree enclosure called the "fish roundabout."

Don't miss the Watkins Hall of Man, with its lifelike scenes of the world's cultural habitats. At the new Earth and Space Hall there's a computerized "shake table" that approximates the intensity of a powerful earthquake, like the one that nearly leveled San Francisco in 1906.

The Japanese Tea Garden, established in 1894, offers something special for all ages: lots of pathways and bridges for inquisitive kids, and fantastic examples of Oriental landscaping and architecture for mom and dad.

Near the park's southeastern corner is the granddaddy of playgrounds. Children's Playground has more than a dozen slides, climbing structures galore and what is arguably California's finest vintage carousel, a turn-of-the-century-era gem that was restored a few years ago.

The San Francisco Zoo

At the San Francisco Zoo (on Sloat near the Great Highway), millions of dollars worth of recent improvements have brought the facility to world-class status. Among the newer attractions are the Primate Discovery Center, Koala Crossing, Gorilla World and Tuxedo Junction penguin pool.

There's also a children's zoo where gentle animals don't mind a hug or pat. Kids under 15 are free when accompanied by an adult.

The Exploratorium

"Don't touch that" is the last thing your kids will hear at the

The most difficult part of a visit to San Francisco's Exploratorium is getting the kids to leave.

Exploratorium, where touching is de rigueur. This hands-on museum of science and human perception holds 600 exhibits that involve visitors in myriad demonstrations ranging from math and motion to smells and sounds.

You'll need reservations to visit the Exploratorium's tactile dome, where only your sense of touch and exploring instinct will lead you through. (The Exploratorium is in the Palace of Fine Arts, 3601 Lyon Street at Marina Boulevard.)

Fort Point

We're often surprised at the number of parents who tell us they've never been to—or ever heard of—Fort Point. One of few west coast Civil War relics, the fort is a great place for kids to absorb some history and let off some steam.

Fortunately, builders of the Golden Gate Bridge spared the historic site, erecting the southernmost support directly above the fort. It has since become a national historic site.

Built between 1853 and 1861 to guard the Golden Gate, Fort Point is a formidable three-tiered structure designed to accommodate 120 cannons and five times as many troops. Tours led by guides in Civil War uniforms help visitors appreciate the life of the Yankee soldiers once stationed here.

For many of our kids who grew up with toys that glorify war games, wandering through the stark halls and the dark jail of Fort Point provides a valuable jolt of reality they'll most certainly learn something from. (The fort is part of the Presidio of San Francisco; take Lincoln Boulevard to Long Avenue.)

Golden Gate Bridge Walk

After visiting the fort, you're in a good position from which to venture out onto the Golden Gate Bridge – on foot.

Although there's a sturdy barrier between sidewalk pedestrians and Marin County–bound traffic, the feeling of zooming autos on one side and the 220-foot drop to the bay on the other can be a bit unnerving. It's an exhilarating (and often windy) walk, and not one for the faint of heart. The pedestrian access is on the San Francisco side of the bridge.

Historic Ships

Just west of Fisherman's Wharf at Pier 43 you'll notice the tall masts of the century-old *Balclutha*, a beautiful Scottish square-rigger that's open for self-guided tours.

Visitors can take a turn at the wheel and relive the Barbary Coast days by prowling the decks and downstairs museum. The captain's quarters, with authentic furnishings and swinging bed, will fascinate landlubbers of all ages.

An assortment of fully restored historic vessels is on view at nearby Hyde Street Pier. They include a three-masted lumber schooner, side-wheel ferry, a scow schooner and two authentic steam tugs.

Before your sea legs give out, herd your group toward Pier 45 at Fisherman's Wharf, where the World War II submarine U.S.S. *Pampanito* is open for tours. The S.S. *Jeremiah O'Brien*, an unaltered World War II "Liberty Ship," is berthed (and open for tours) at Fort Mason, Pier 3.

Pier 39 Waterfront Marketplace

It's definitely there for the tourists, but let's face it: Pier 39, with all its glitz, has definite family appeal. With more than two dozen eateries, many of them with very reasonable prices, Pier 39 is a great place to satisfy nearly every gastronomic craving—while staying within a tight family budget.

The 100-plus specialty shops are likewise bound to offer something for just about everyone. We found a kite shop, an NFL shop, a puzzle shop, a Christmas shop, a magnet shop, a magic shop and a kids' wear boutique.

There's also a double-decker carousel and regularly scheduled shows by street musicians, jugglers and mimes. (Pier 39 is along the Embarcadero.)

Alcatraz

When I was growing up, Alcatraz Prison could only be toured in my imagination. I can still recall looking out over the Bay and conjuring up mental pictures of the nasty criminals who spent years in exile out there.

Since then the National Park Service has opened the former federal prison to visitors. Guided tours now pass through cell blocks, and the grounds are open to explorations on your own.

Alcatraz tour cruises leave from Pier 41, and advance reservations through Ticketron are advised.

Cable Cars

For visiting families, seeing San Francisco without riding a cable car is like eating apple pie without ice cream. It's good, but something's missing.

Besides being a functional form of transportation, the cable cars are the city's most popular tourist attraction, carrying 14 million passengers every year.

Veteran riders will tell you the most spectacular rides are to be had on the Powell-Hyde line. That is, if you enjoy hills so steep that conductors often holler "Heeere we go!" as they begin their descent. The cars run between the Powell and Market street intersection and Victorian Park on Hyde Street, a block from Ghirardelli Square. Best (and most popular) seats are along the outside.

The place where the city's cable car fleet sleeps is another kid pleaser. The Car Barn Powerhouse and Cable Car Museum (Washington and Mason streets) serves as the system's hub. On view, in addition to the original 1873 cable car and other memorabilia, are the winding gear and cables that carry the vehicles up and down the hills. A glass-enclosed room offers a bird's-eye view of the steel cable moving through large sheaves to the streets.

Dessert

Judging by the ever-present crowds, the Ghirardelli Chocolate Manufactory (at Ghirardelli Square) ranks high on San Francisco's list of musts. One reviewer referred to this historic soda fountain and candy shop as a weight-watcher's Waterloo.

Spending the Night?

The Sheraton at Fisherman's Wharf, TraveLodge at the Wharf and Holiday Inn at Fisherman's Wharf have cribs and rollaways, as well as outdoor pools and indoor movies. Children (age restrictions vary) stay free in their parents' room. Expensive. All three are close to numerous attractions, including the cable cars, Pier 39, the historic ships and Ghirardelli Square.

San Jose

Like Fresno and Bakersfield, which have their share of identity problems, San Jose is used to jabs and jokes. However, even the most skeptical would have difficulty naming many other California cities that rival San Jose in the breadth of activities available for families.

Rosicrucian Museum

A little slice of Egypt in the midst of Silicon Valley, the Rosicrucian Museum holds the western United States' most extensive array of Egyptian, Assyrian and Babylonian artifacts.

Among the most intriguing is a collection of mummies: adults, children and animals. There are also detailed models of both the Rosetta Stone and the Temple of Ramses the Great.

Although there are more than two thousand artifacts on display here, kids, being kids, will probably be drawn to the mummies and to a macabre collection of South American shrunken heads. (The museum is at Park and Naglee avenues.)

Happy Hollow Park and Zoo

This 12-acre wonderland entices children with a giant carousel, real pygmy animals, puppet shows, petting zoo and even a ride through a bamboo forest on "Danny the Dragon." (Find it at Keyes and Senter roads.)

Winchester Mystery House

Stairways that climb nowhere, doors leading into blank walls, 160 weird rooms in all. . . . To say the home's creator, Sarah Winchester, was odd is quite an understatement. Heiress to the Winchester rifle fortune and obsessed with the occult, Sarah (and a cadre of carpenters laboring 24 hours a day) worked for 38 years on this sprawling Victorian mansion.

The $5 million "mystery house," as it came to be known, is listed on the National Register of Historic Places. It's also the site of a large collection of firearms and antique products manufactured by the Winchester company. (It's at 525 S. Winchester Boulevard.)

World of Miniature

No, you haven't landed in Lilliput. This is World of Miniature, where rural towns, railroads and switchyards all sit under one roof (1375 S. Bascom Avenue.) Most of the displays here are one-inch-to-

A visit to the Rosicrucian Museum is like a step into ancient Egypt.

one-foot scale models, and all are exquisitely detailed. You'll begin to think you're Gulliver.

Grant Ranch Stables

This is a working ranch that welcomes visitors. Activities include horseback riding, hay rides and fishing. It's at 18415 Mount Hamilton Road; call (408) 274-9258 for hours and directions.

Spending the Night?

The Hyatt San Jose and Red Lion Motor Inn both have pools, whirlpools and jogging paths. The Holiday Inn–Park Center Plaza and Howard Johnson's Motor Lodge both offer "family plans." Moderate to Expensive.

The
Central Coast

❦

Santa Cruz

❦ The Monterey Peninsula has Pebble Beach, Carmel, Clint Eastwood and some of the world's most spectacular coastal scenery. But Santa Cruz has the sun. Many's the time we've lounged on a sunny Santa Cruz County beach while a bank of fog blanketed the peninsula across the bay. Locals call this place "the sunny side of the bay."

The Santa Cruz Beach Boardwalk (see separate listing in Part II, Theme Parks) and its mile-long beach may draw the lion's share of the city's tourists, but the Santa Cruz area has much more to offer.

The municipal wharf stretches into the bay from one end of the Boardwalk's beach. A favorite fishing hangout, the wharf is also home to sea lions that bask on the wood pilings above the waves. They're usually visible through openings at the end of the wharf. (Just follow the barking.)

Natural Bridges State Beach (at the end of West Cliff Drive), although not the safest spot for swimming, is equipped with nice picnic facilities. If you visit between October and March, be sure to take the short trail for a look at the thousands of monarch butterflies that cover the trees and flutter about.

Harvey West Park is one of the town's best-kept secrets. Near the intersection of Highways 9 and 1 in the west part of Santa Cruz, the park sits at the edge of a beautiful grove of trees. You'll find a public pool, old train engine for climbing, lots of play equipment, softball fields and picnic areas. Oceanview Park (at the end of Oceanview) has creative play equipment and a nice view of the Boardwalk.

Three miles north of town on Branciforte Drive is a Mystery Spot, one of those weird places where gravity plays tricks. A bit farther from town in Felton, off Graham Hill Road, the Roaring Camp and Big Trees Railroad runs vintage steam-train excursions through redwood forests. The company also offers train trips (in open cars) between Roaring Camp and Santa Cruz.

If it's sun and sand you've come for, we suggest you forsake the crowded Boardwalk beach for more pleasant environs. Here are some alternatives.

The nice little beach in front of the Dream Inn adjacent to the wharf is often overlooked, despite its proximity to the Boardwalk.

The sandy beach between the San Lorenzo River and yacht harbor is also a good bet. Twin Lakes State Beach is on the east side of the harbor.

Finding a parking space in downtown Capitola on a sunny day is about as easy as winning the California Lottery, but the expansive beach here, with its gentle wave action, is worth the short hike from the adjacent neighborhoods where parking is more plentiful.

As a general rule of thumb, the farther east you drive from the Boardwalk, the less crowded the beaches are likely to be. Exceptions are the state beaches of New Brighton and Seacliff, which get their share of visitors (and charge fees). The beaches from Rio del Mar south are often the least crowded.

Surfing and boogie-board enthusiasts opt for Steamer Lane (south of the wharf), Pleasure Point (near the end of 41st Avenue) and Manresa Beach (near La Selva Beach). There are surfboard and boogie-board rental shops close to all the popular wave-riding spots.

Spending the Night?

Santa Cruz has thus far resisted several attempts to build large-scale, full-service resort complexes. But there are plenty of comfortable motels throughout the area.

The Dream Inn, which overlooks the municipal wharf, is the most prominent. All rooms have bay views, and it's a short walk to the Boardwalk. Expensive.

Also in Santa Cruz, about three blocks from the beach, is the Best Western Torch-Lite Inn. Moderate.

The Best Western Sea Cliff Inn in Aptos next to Highway 1 is among the newer mid-county motels. A state beach is just over the highway. Moderate.

The Capitola Inn is also situated next to Highway 1, a healthy walk from Capitola Village. Moderate.

All the above have swimming pools.

Monterey Peninsula

🐭 World-famous golf courses, a picture-postcard coastline, quaint Carmel. . . . Probably no other area in California gets as much attention as the Monterey Peninsula.

While sometimes it seems that every tourist in America is competing with you for a parking place here, something special keeps drawing back visitors, including our family, time and time again.

Since swimming conditions are generally unsafe (with cold water, unpredictable riptides and cross currents) along this part of the California coast, the beach often takes a back seat to dry-land family activities—some well known, others more obscure.

Monterey

California's "other" Fisherman's Wharf is always a pleasant diversion. The open-air markets display quite a variety of fresh, edible sea life, many of them rather exotic species that will intrigue the kids.

Having grown up with TV's "Zorro," I've always been fascinated by the historical section of town, where buildings from the Spanish occupation conjure up visions of the masked man jumping from balcony to balcony. Many of the vintage buildings, including Colton Hall (where the California Constitution was drafted), are open for exploring. These sites are spread over a wide area downtown, so it's a good idea to pick up a tour map from the Chamber of Commerce on Alvarado Street.

Dennis the Menace Playground (at El Estero Park off Del Monte

San Carlos Borromeo in Carmel is one of the most popular stops along California's "mission trail."

Avenue) is one of the best in Northern California, according to our young playground connoisseurs. Hank Ketchum, a former local resident and creator of the "Dennis" comics, designed some of the equipment. There's a swinging bridge, an old train locomotive, tunnels, a hedge maze and lots and lots of sand.

On your stroll down Cannery Row—or what's left of it—drop by the Edgewater Packing Company (on Wave Street). Tucked inside are a carousel and goodie shop.

The Monterey Bay Aquarium (on the west end of Cannery Row) became an overnight tourist sensation when it opened a few years ago. After all, where else can you come face to face with otters, octopi and wolf eels? Children also get a kick out of the bat-ray petting pool and touch tide pool.

To avoid the crowds, the best time to visit the aquarium is morning. You'll need advance reservations: call (408) 375-3333.

Pacific Grove

Just beyond Cannery Row is the old community of Pacific Grove, where restored Victorians line the narrow residential streets and the pace is decidedly slow.

At the northern tip of the peninsula is Point Piños Lighthouse (at Lighthouse Avenue and Asilomar Boulevard). California's oldest operating lighthouse is often open for tours and is worth a look-see.

In late October, the monarch butterflies descend upon this area. George Washington Park and Butterfly Trees Lodge are good places to view them.

Carmel

The only way to truly appreciate this forever-quaint village is on foot. That is, if you can find a place to park. Carmel's white sand beach, at the foot of Ocean Avenue, is a great place to park the troops for a picnic or a romp along the water's edge.

Mission San Carlos Borromeo (take Rio Road off Highway 1) is full of California history: American Indian items, religious artifacts, the state's first library and re-creations of 18th-century rooms. Father Junipero Serra, who established the California missions, is entombed here.

Spending the Night?

Walking into the Sundial Lodge (Monte Verde and Seventh Avenue) in downtown Carmel is like stepping into a fairy tale. With its storybook facade, the Sundial is a fitting addition to the quaint architecture of Carmel. The rooms have kitchen nooks, and there are a few suites. Moderate.

The Hyatt Regency Monterey has close to six hundred rooms, a pool and tennis courts. Expensive. The Doubletree Hotel is a full-service facility (with swimming and tennis) near Fisherman's Wharf. Expensive.

For a listing of more than a hundred peninsula hotels and motels, write to the Monterey Peninsula Chamber of Commerce and Visitors Bureau at P.O. Box 1770, Monterey, CA 93940.

Asilomar
PACIFIC GROVE

❦ The secret's out. You don't have to be part of a big group to enjoy the seaside setting (and affordable rates) of Asilomar Conference Center. Yes, you will find plenty of folks running around with name tags and briefcases. This is one of California's preeminent conference destinations. But chances are you'll also run into an occasional family enjoying a meal in the dining hall or lounging by the pool.

A unit of the state park system, Asilomar is set among one hundred natural acres of forest, dune and beach at the tip of Monterey Peninsula. It's not uncommon to see deer and raccoons wandering around the dozens of shingled lodge units, which blend nicely with the environs.

Guests at Asilomar have access to a pool (heated year-round), horseshoe pits, volleyball courts and an exercise trail. The white, mile-long Asilomar State Beach is a short stroll through the trees. The conference center will make golf, tennis, fishing and tour arrangements for you as well. Some lodge units back right up to the beach, and many have water views.

The Phoebe Hearst Social Hall, with its large fireplace, Ping-Pong

Some lucky Asilomar guests have ocean views.

and pool tables, and grand piano, is a popular indoor gathering place, especially when the fog rolls in, as it often does here.

For those venturing into Carmel, to the Monterey Bay Aquarium or other points of interest, the local bus service makes stops at Asilomar.

Table d'hôte service (lunch and dinner from a predetermined menu) is also available in the dining room. Asilomar bakes its own tempting bread and desserts.

Asilomar Conference Center, 800 Asilomar Boulevard (P.O. Box 537), Pacific Grove, CA 93950. Telephone (408) 372-8016. From Highway 1, between Carmel and Monterey, drive west on Highway 68 and proceed to the Asilomar gate posts at the end of the highway. Three hundred thirteen rooms. Cribs and rollaways available. Full breakfast included. Special rates for children. Inexpensive to expensive.

Valley Lodge

CARMEL VALLEY

❦ No, this isn't quaint Carmel-by-the-Sea. Carmel Valley, just a short drive from "the other one," is a small community nestled among the coastal foothills in a valley that stretches inland from the ocean.

After a day of browsing and ambling along the coast, the Valley Lodge offers visitors the opportunity to unwind and stretch in a more quiet, rural setting.

A small resort, the lodge has only 31 rooms. But it's big on facilities for families. Summer days can be mighty warm up here, and the Valley Lodge is equipped with the requisite pool. There's also a fitness center with weights, stationary bike and mini-trampoline, as well as a game area with Ping-Pong, horseshoes and spa. Across the street is a park with a playground, and tennis courts are a block away.

Accommodations range from garden-patio rooms to one- and two-bedroom cottages with fireplaces and kitchens. On the patios are firewood and barbeques.

Guests are served a continental breakfast every morning and receive a copy of the newspaper of their choice. Just don't hog the funnies.

Valley Lodge, Carmel Valley Road at Ford Road (P.O. Box 93), Carmel Valley, CA 93924. Telephone (408) 659-2261. From Highway 1 in Carmel, drive east on Carmel Valley Road 11 miles to the lodge at Ford Road. Thirty-one patio and cottage rooms, some with fireplaces and kitchens. Cribs and rollaways available. Pool, spa, sauna, game area, fitness room; park with playground and tennis nearby. Continental breakfast included. Moderate to expensive.

Diversions

See Monterey Peninsula listing, above.

The Mother Lode

❦

Apple Hill
EL DORADO COUNTY

❦ Every fall, when El Dorado County's apple trees begin to sag under the weight of their fruit, the annual crush of hungry visitors isn't far behind. For tens of thousands of Sacramento Valley families, a pilgrimage to the ranches and orchards of Apple Hill has become as much a ritual as a trip to the hills for a cut-your-own Christmas tree.

This fall festival was the brainchild of a group of about 50 ranchers who, from around harvest time (September or October) through early November, entice apple lovers to the foothills with entertainment, rides, rich desserts, colorful foliage and lots and lots of apples.

Over the years, our family has chosen a few favorite ranches, but every year there seems to be a new one serving up some neat apple dessert.

For most visitors, the first stop after leaving Highway 50 (just above Placerville) is High Hill Ranch, unofficial king of the festival. There are craft booths with lots of country knickknacks, a large produce area, well-stocked trout pond (pay for your catch by the pound) and a shed where you can watch workers press apples into fresh juice.

Another favorite is Kids Inc., a rustic outpost that has people lined up out the door waiting for a locally famous "walkin' pie" or huge slice of apple pie à la mode. (A hungry six-footer in our group couldn't finish his generous helping.) A sizable pumpkin patch awaits visitors on the hill behind Kids Inc.

Other Apple Hill participants include El Dorado Orchards, which operates a short train ride for kids, and the Apple Pantry, offering carriage rides.

Along the way are numerous other ranches selling a variety of apples and apple desserts: strudel, fritters, donuts, butter squares, crepes, muffins, and on and on.

While hot meals can be purchased at many of the ranches, we prefer to bring a picnic lunch and spread our blanket on the grass under a tree or at tables provided by a number of growers. A good picnic spot is at O'Halloran's Apple Train Ranch, with its nice lawn area and nature trail.

To reach Apple Hill, drive east from Sacramento on Highway 50. Our advice is to take the Carson exit (about 10 minutes past Placerville) and begin your tour at High Hill ranch. There you can rest, browse and pick up a free Apple Hill map for plotting the rest of your tour. You may also request a copy in advance by sending a self-addressed, stamped envelope to the Apple Hill Growers, P.O. Box 494, Camino, CA 95709.

Diversions

If you're coming from Sacramento on Highway 50, Sam's Town at Shingle Springs is a great place for a rest stop. The building facades resemble a Gold Rush–era community, and inside are restaurants and gift shops. A curious assortment of vehicles is sprinkled about the grounds. The city of Placerville operates Gold Bug Mine (in Bedford Park), where you can poke along a lengthy, lighted shaft that operated until the 1940's.

Spending the Night?

Stagecoach Motor Inn, at the end of the Apple Hill Trail in Pollack Pines, has family suites and kitchenettes. The River Rock Inn in Placerville offers bed and breakfast on the American River. Kids are welcome, and are invited to pan for gold in the front yard.

Llamahall
Guest Ranch
S O N O R A

❦ A century or so ago, hordes of prospectors packing shovels and harboring dreams of riches invaded the Mother Lode in search of buried fortunes. Although the Gold Rush is long since over, this region is still a gold mine of sorts for families interested in staking a recreational claim. Skiing, cave exploring, poking around Gold Rush ruins, water sports . . . it's all here.

The gold country has long been a favorite destination of ours, but we've been somewhat disappointed with the area's lack of interesting family accommodations. That is until we stumbled upon Llamahall Guest Ranch, outside Sonora. In a region dotted with dime-a-dozen motels, this back-road retreat is a breath of fresh air.

Resident ducks are the first to greet visitors to the ranch. A few yards up the driveway a family of llamas stare as the occasional car lumbers by.

Innkeeper Cindy Hall, who shares the billing with her llamas, raises these friendly beasts, which also serve as diversions for visitors. (Guests are invited to feed and walk the animals.)

Accommodations are in the lower tier of the large, multilevel family home where two large rooms (with private baths) have been set aside for guests. Unfortunately, only one room is set up to accommodate families, making a reservation a must. A hallway between the two rooms holds a small refrigerator and phone.

Guests also have access to the home's oak-panelled "music room" with an antique piano, assorted instruments, games and a fireplace. The adjacent deck holds a spa and sauna. Breakfast is served in the dining room.

The wooded grounds offer children's play equipment, hiking trails, Indian grinding rocks, a pond for fishing and a year-round creek where kids and parents can try their hand at gold panning. The forty-niners never had it this good.

Llamahall Guest Ranch, 18170 Wards Ferry Road, Sonora, CA 95370. Telephone (209) 532-7264. From Sonora, drive east on Highway 108 for two-and-a-half miles. Turn right on Tuolumne Road and right on Wards Ferry Road. Then go right at the Llamahall sign to the ranch. Two rooms, both with bath. Breakfast included. Moderate to expensive.

Diversions

The Dodge Ridge ski area, a family favorite, is about 30 miles away, as is Pinecrest Lake, a pristine Sierra jewel. Water skiers flock to nearby Melones Reservoir. Don't miss nearby Columbia State Historic Park, also nearby (and subject of a listing of its own in Part II). There are also public cave tours in the vicinity (check the Caves and Caverns section of Part III). Ask at the ranch about Tuolumne River raft trips.

The Lake Tahoe Region

❦

Sorensen's

HOPE VALLEY

❦ One of the best-kept secrets of the Lake Tahoe region is Hope Valley, along Carson Pass in Alpine County. California's pioneers crossed this area on their way through the Sierra to the Sacramento Valley.

Among the early settlers were the Sorensens, a Danish farm family who homesteaded sheep-grazing land here a century ago. Around 1915, the family began renting their sheepherders' cabins to fishermen, thereby establishing one of the oldest resorts in the region. In fact, one of those early cabins is still in use.

Sorensen's has seen a growth spurt recently, thanks to the Brissenden family who operate the 165-acre, year-round resort. Some 20 cabins – both old and new – are set amid glistening aspen in the lush valley.

If the bikes (belonging to the Brissenden children) parked in front of the family residence don't convince you that families are welcome here, the list of activities will. When snow isn't covering the ground, kids can play along the brook that flows through the property, toss horseshoes or take advantage of a collection of games and puzzles stacked in the office. There's even a pint-sized log-walled playhouse.

Special family-oriented seasonal activities include guided walking tours along portions of the old Emigrant Trail (the longest hike

Lodging at Sorensen's ranges from old, rustic cabins to modern log units like Creekside.

is about a mile); various ski packages offered through Kirkwood ski resort, about a half-hour drive away; and river rafting down the nearby east fork of the Carson River. For cross-country skiers, Sorensen's has marked more than 10 kilometers of trails.

Accommodations are available for families of all sizes (and budgets). Our cabin, called Creekside, was among more recent additions to the resort. The pine log cabin is equipped with bathroom, kitchen facilities, a wood stove, double bed and a sleeping loft, which, during our visit, served alternately as a fort and doll nursery. A wide, cushioned window seat fit two children in sleeping bags.

Those who don't prepare meals in their cabins (most have kitchenettes) shouldn't expect to find much in the way of dining alternatives out here in sparsely populated Hope Valley. Other than the cafe at Sorensen's (which serves good food), the closest restaurant is several miles east at Woolfords.

In addition to their considerable work in upgrading the historic resort, the Brissendens should be commended for an enforced ban on indoor smoking at Sorensen's. Says their brochure, "We pride ourselves on the freshness and cleanliness of our cabins, but we can't keep them that way after someone's spent a weekend chain smoking." Three cheers for clean air!

Sorensen's, Highway 89, Hope Valley, CA 96120. Telephone (916) 694-2203. From Highway 50 at Myers, drive south on Highway 88 for 11 miles. Turn left at the 88/89 junction. Sorensen's is about a half mile up the road. Twenty housekeeping cabins (which sleep from two to eight people), all with baths, most with kitchen facilities. Moderate to expensive.

Lakeland Village
SOUTH LAKE TAHOE

❦ This is one of those resorts that people often overlook on the way to the gaming tables and slot machines of Stateline. Although Lakeland Village sits along Lake Tahoe's most congested boulevard, it gets our vote as the area's best family resort.

What casino-bound passersby don't see are the resort's vast, well-manicured grounds that back up against a thousand-foot-long sandy beach. (The highway might as well be a million miles away.)

In addition to the beach, guests have full run of a recreation area that includes two swimming pools, wading pool, tennis courts, summer game room, kids' play equipment, spa and saunas. Laundry facilities are also on-site.

Accommodations (there are more than two hundred units in all) are varied. Besides the one-bedroom suites in the main lodge, there are clusters of one-, two-, three- and four-bedroom townhouses (with fireplaces), completely furnished, down to the kitchen utensils.

Lakeland Village, 3535 Lake Tahoe Boulevard (P.O. Box A), South Lake Tahoe, CA 95705. Telephone, toll-free in California, (800) 822-5969. Studios, suites and townhouses; complete kitchens, fireplaces. Cribs and rollaways available. Pools, play equipment, game room, tennis, spa, saunas, rental rafts, paddleboats and canoes. Moderate to expensive.

Diversions

One of the only reasons for leaving the resort is food. Lakeland Village has no restaurants, but they are plentiful in the immediate area. While people under age 21 can't enjoy Nevada's gaming action, some of the nearby casinos do allow children into their restaurants and dinner shows. Getting a peek into this fascinating adults-only world can be quite an adventure for children. There's a miniature golf course just south of Lakeland Village, next to the Upper Truckee River on Highway 50.

Camp Richardson
SOUTH LAKE TAHOE

❦ This is one of those resorts the kids' grandparents might remember. Venerable Camp Richardson has been around, in one form or another, since the 1920's, and is one of the south shore's oldest retreats.

When Alonzo Richardson began building cabins here, he named them after vintage autos like Stutz and Pierce Arrow. Later proprietors have carried on the tradition, but the newer cabins bear more contemporary names, like Thunderbird and El Dorado. In all, more than three dozen cabins, all with private bath and fully equipped kitchens, share the resort's 80-plus pine-studded acres between Highway 89 and the lake.

Owned by the government and run by a private operator, Camp Richardson has retained its rustic ambience, despite rampant development of the south-shore area. It's a nice place to get away from the hustle and bustle of South Lake Tahoe but close enough to practice "elbow exercises" if the urge strikes.

Activities include horseshoes, Ping-Pong, tennis, a small playground, volleyball and croquet. There's a lifeguard on duty at the private beach during summer months. More recent additions to the camp include a lakefront restaurant and marina.

Camp Richardson, Highway 89 (P.O. Box 10648), South Lake Tahoe, CA 95731. Telephone (916) 541-1801. More than three dozen cabins, all with private bath and kitchen facilities. Private beach, play area and games. Moderate to expensive.

Diversions

Mom and dad (while the kids played in the woods) were intrigued with the Tallac Historic Site next to the resort. The U.S. government maintains a complex of mansions built between 1894 and 1923 by wealthy vacationers. Guided tours give you a glimpse of how the upper crust enjoyed summers at the lake long ago. Just north of the mansions off Highway 89 is the Lake Tahoe Forest Visitors Center, which is a kind of hub for a series of easy trails that head off in various directions. The quarter-mile path to the Stream Profile Chamber is a good choice, especially if young children are along. Visitors here get a fish-eye view of Taylor Creek and its aquatic life, including the salmon run, during the fall. Along the trail are various hands-on ecological points of interest. There's also an easy bike trail that runs along this portion of Highway 89.

Meeks Bay Resort
TAHOE CITY

❦ This rustic summer resort, located below Tahoe City on the western shore, offers single- and two-story cottages and lake-front condos sleeping as many as seven. All are available only on a weekly basis from June through September.

If you've got a large brood, Meeks Bay is a good choice. A two-story cottage, for example, has a living room, two bedrooms, bath, fully equipped kitchen, observation dining porch and lake view.

For extra large groups the resort also rents out the Kehlet Mansion, a seven-bedroom, three-bath home that sleeps as many as 12.

The lake is never more than a short walk away, regardless of where you stay at the resort. When you tire of lounging on the beach, the office here rents bikes for exploration of the area. There's also an ice cream parlor.

The resort's own marina, one of Tahoe's most sheltered, operates from late May through October. There are two launching ramps. For those just passing through, the private beach at Meeks Bay Resort (along with play equipment) can be enjoyed on a day-use basis for a reasonable fee.

Meeks Bay Resort, P.O. Box 7979 (the address from May through October), Tahoe City, CA 95730. Telephone (916) 525-7242. Ten miles south of Tahoe City and 17 miles north of South Lake Tahoe on Highway 89. Cottages and condos. Rollaways and cribs available. Private beach, children's play area. Moderate to expensive (weekly).

Granlibakken

TAHOE CITY

🍎 Set among the pines about a mile from busy Highway 89, Granlibakken is one of the north shore's secluded gems. Regardless of the time of year, there's always something fun going on here.

When we dropped by during a winter weekend, the resort's very own ski hill and snow play area were alive with visiting families. Moms and dads looking for an uncrowded area (away from the hot-doggers) to introduce their children to skiing often look to Granlibakken's more gentle slopes. And with ski rentals and lift tickets included in your lodging rate, the price is certainly right. Lessons are also available. (For more seasoned skiers, Alpine Meadows, Homewood, Tahoe Ski Bowl and Squaw Valley are nearby.)

No sooner does the snow melt when out come the tennis togs and swim suits. Granlibakken has an indoor pool, children's wading pool, jogging trail and eight tennis courts. The resort is also close to golf, hiking trails, rafting on the Truckee River and boating and swimming at the lake.

The 115 European-style one-, two- and three-bedroom condo units are all privately owned, and each is furnished like a home away from home. Most have kitchens and many have fireplaces, lofts, patios or decks.

About the only service you won't find on the grounds is a restaurant. But with Tahoe City only a mile or so away, visitors won't go hungry.

Granlibakken Ski and Racquet Resort, P.O. Box 6329, Tahoe City, CA 95730. Telephone (916) 583-4242. From Tahoe City, drive south on

Highway 89 (the lakeside highway) for a half mile. Turn right on Granlibakken Road and follow for about one mile to resort. One hundred fifteen one-, two- and three-bedroom units, many with kitchens and fireplaces. Cribs and rollaways available. Ski area and snow play area on-site. Moderate to expensive.

Tahoe Sands Resort

TAHOE VISTA

❦ Like neighboring Franciscan Lakeside Lodge, Tahoe Sands Resort is divided by the north-shore highway and consists of wood-side and lakeside units.

The lakeside Lanai Building has rooms that sleep from two to four people. We were most impressed, however, with the lakeside cottages that look out over Lake Tahoe. These four-person units have queen and twin beds, living room, full kitchens and wood stoves.

Along the lengthy private beach are swings, picnic tables and kayaks, which are available to guests. There's also a pool that's enclosed during the winter.

Tahoe Sands Resort, 6610 North Lake Boulevard, Tahoe Vista, CA 95732. Telephone (916) 546-2592. Motel and cottage units, some with kitchens. Pool, private beach, children's play area. Moderate to expensive.

Franciscan Lakeside Lodge

TAHOE VISTA

❦ This tidy complex actually sits on both sides of busy Highway 28 (Lake Boulevard). On the lake side, you'll pay a few dollars more but won't have to worry about children crossing traffic to get to the beach. (Unfortunately, the pool is on the mountain side of the street.)

Lakefront cabins (studios and one and two bedrooms) sit smack on the glistening private beach. These units have decks for sunning

Some of Tahoe's lakeside resorts have shallow, well-marked water play areas.

or watching the kids and are equipped with kitchens that have stove, oven, dishwasher, pots, pans and cutlery.

At one end of the grounds are swings, volleyball area, horseshoe pit and picnic tables. The lodge also has its own pier. There's a recreation park with tennis courts nearby.

Franciscan Lakeside Lodge, 6944 North Lake Boulevard, Tahoe Vista, CA 95732. Telephone (916) 546-7234. Lakefront and lakeview units and cabins, pool, private beach, children's play area. Rollaways available. Moderate to expensive.

Northstar-at-Tahoe

TRUCKEE

❦ It's only a few minutes by car to Tahoe, but during a visit to Northstar the lake's lure temporarily takes a back seat. With the variety of diversions available at this year-round resort, you'll not likely be too tempted to break away.

With access to miles of trails, golf course, 10 tennis courts, huge pools, two spas, exercise/game room, fitness course and riding stables, families are anything but bored. And during the winter there's skiing at one of the north shore's better resorts. (Northstar also operates a cross-country and telemark ski center.)

The folks at Northstar were among the first north-state resorts to offer an innovation they call Minor's Camp. For slightly more than we pay our own babysitter to watch our TV, guests age 2 to 10 can enroll in a supervised program that transcends traditional day care. Minor's Camp activities include nature walks, water play, cooking, art, drama and science. Winter Minor's Campers can take advantage of Northstar's "PeeWee" ski option, consisting of an hour-and-a-half morning ski lesson.

The Minor's Camp is located in the Village Plaza area of the resort. This is Northstar's hub. Restaurants (including a pizza parlor), a general store, video store, deli, ski shop and the recreation center are all situated here.

It's good to keep this in mind when booking your reservation. Northstar has more than two hundred lodging units, from hotel-type rooms at the village to plush condos and homes, some located quite a ways from all the activities. For those out of walking range, Northstar runs an intraresort shuttle service to and from the village.

My group found a village lodge room, while not as peaceful and quiet as the condos and homes outside the village, more than adequate, as we were only steps away from all the fun and could come and go when we wanted.

Units can sleep up to 10. All except lodge rooms have kitchens and fireplaces.

Rental guests have full run of the extensive recreation center, and can take advantage of various golf or ski package deals. Fitness classes such as outdoor body conditioning and aquatic pool exercise are also offered for men and women.

Northstar-at-Tahoe, P.O. Box 2499, Truckee, CA 95734. Telephone, toll-free in California, (800) 822-5987. From downtown Truckee, drive south on Highway 267 for six miles. Rental office is adjacent to highway. From Kings Beach (North Lake Tahoe), drive north on Highway 267. More than two hundred units, from lodge rooms to homes. Many require multinight stay minimums. Child care, recreation center, skiing, stables, tennis. Restaurants on-site. Moderate to expensive.

Yosemite
National Park

❧

About Yosemite

❧ Even kids who reserve their oohs and ahhs for the latest adolescent heart throb or the most thoroughly disgusting toy action figure will likely drop their jaws while standing most anywhere in Yosemite Valley, taking in the 360-degree view of gleaming granite and glistening waterfalls. Although such visual delights, especially in combination with a relaxing lounge chair, are sufficient to keep many a parent pacified for hours, nature seems to hold young children's attention typically as long as homework that's done in front of the TV during an episode of "The Cosby Show." Therefore, parents will appreciate the fact that Yosemite has a great deal more going for it than the most captivating scenery in California—maybe in the world.

Regardless of the season, there's always something fun to do in this most popular of California's national parks. During the warm months there's rafting in the Merced River, swimming in park pools, horseback and bike riding and short or long family hikes. In the wintertime, skaters hit the outdoor ice rink at Camp Curry and skiers take to the slopes at Badger Pass.

Accommodations in the park are as varied as visitors' budgets. At the inexpensive end are the campgrounds as well as the canvas-covered housekeeping cabins at Camp Curry. Next up is Yosemite Lodge, offering a choice of rustic cabins or more modern rooms. At the top end is the pricey and popular Ahwahnee Hotel, where a bellman brings in the bags.

No matter where you choose to stay in the park, plan your Yosemite visit well in advance. If you reserve lodging months – even a year – before your trip, you're more likely to get what you want and where you want it. The advance work will be well worth it.

Yosemite Lodge

YOSEMITE
NATIONAL PARK

❦ If a tent is a bit too primitive but shelling out $150 for a room at the Ahwahnee Hotel will send you foraging for acorns and berries at dinner time, Yosemite Lodge is a comfortable compromise.

Reasonably priced accommodations here range from small, clean cabins with or without baths to modern motel-type units scattered around the grounds. We've tried both and found each to have its advantages. While the motel units have the most conveniences, the walls between rooms are thin, and we got to know our neighbors even though we never met. The cabins, while spartan, offer more privacy. (Rollaways and cribs are available.)

For family activities, we found Yosemite Lodge and the area around it to offer the most. The short trail to Yosemite Falls starts just across the road, and the Merced River flows a short walk away. Nature programs are offered (indoors and outdoors) on many evenings during the year.

The lodge also operates a bicycle rental shop, which is particularly appealing to families. Bikes with child carriers and helmets are plentiful, and lengthy sections of paved trails have been created for cyclists. For relaxing, the lodge has what is arguably the best swimming pool in the valley.

Parents will enjoy parking the car upon arrival and leaving it until departing. Unless you're planning a trip out of the valley, you can rely on free shuttle busses that run daily. Visitors are discouraged from using their cars. (Busses even make winter runs up to the Badger Pass ski area.)

Although a popular collection of restaurants and shops is located in Yosemite Village a quick bus ride or walk away, the lodge operates a small store and a gift shop with Native American crafts. Lodge restaurants met the varied preferences of our finicky group. At the cafeteria you slide your own tray and eat in a large dining hall. The Mountain Room Broiler serves more expensive meat and fish entrees. Our highest rating went to Four Seasons Restaurant for its children's menu, good food and reasonable prices.

If you prefer, the cafeteria (with a day's notice) will pack box lunches so your family can eat in a meadow. The price is right and you can't beat the view.

Yosemite Lodge, Yosemite National Park, CA 95389. Reservations: telephone (209) 252-4848. Yosemite Valley is 81 miles from Merced on Highway 140. Four hundred eighty-four units (cabins with bath or without bath; central shower facilities available) and modern lodge rooms with private baths. Cribs and rollaways available. Economical learn-to-ski mid-week packages are offered during the winter. Less expensive to moderate.

Diversions

Activities include bike rentals and swimming pool (at the lodge); nature walks (throughout the valley); ice skating (Camp Curry during winter); skiing (Badger Pass during winter); horse, pony and mule riding (Valley Stables); six-hour burro picnic for children from 7 to 12 years (Valley Stables); sightseeing tours; Indian Cultural Museum (Visitor Center); innertubing and rafting on the Merced River; playground (village school and Ahwahnee Hotel); year-round Junior Ranger program for kids (Visitor Center); camera walks (Ansel Adams Gallery); evening ranger programs (various locales); children's hour and Yosemite Theater performing and film programs (Visitor Center). The view from Glacier Point is well worth the drive, and views of Lower Yosemite Falls, Bridalveil Falls and Mirror Lake are worth the short hikes.

Ahwahnee Hotel

YOSEMITE
NATIONAL PARK

❦ Unlike many higher-priced hotels, where the parking lots are filled with European sports cars and fancy sedans, Yosemite's Ahwahnee plays host to a diverse clientele. From international jet-setters who ooze wealth as they stroll through the lobby to middle-class families from the Central Valley who've saved their nickels and dimes for months, the Ahwahnee's guest list represents a happy melting pot.

One of California's grandest hotels (a national historic landmark, at that), this venerable stone and wood fortress has entertained Yosemite visitors since 1927, when rates were $15 to $20. (The nightly tariff was hovering around $150 at this writing.)

The years have been good to the Ahwahnee. A restoration a few years ago (in anticipation of a visit by Queen Elizabeth) preserved the tasteful American Indian ornamentation that sets the hotel apart from any other. With old basketry and weavings on display throughout the public areas, the Ahwahnee has the trappings of a Native American shrine. The soaring ceilings and playhouse-sized fireplace of the Great Lounge even commanded the respect of our kids, who lowered their vocal intensity a decibel or two out of respect.

The lion's share of rooms are under the main hotel roof, but many visitors are surprised to discover a cluster of 26 homey cottages, which afford families a bit more space and privacy, as well as easier access to the great outdoors.

While this grand resort is not particularly set up to cater to young families, the Ahwahnee does have a swimming pool and game room.

Ahwahnee Hotel, Yosemite National Park, CA 95389. Reservations: telephone (209) 252-4848. Yosemite Valley is 81 miles from Merced on Highway 140. Ninety-seven rooms and 26 cottages, all with baths. Cribs and rollaways available. Pool, tennis and children's play area. Restaurant on-site and others nearby. Expensive.

Diversions

See listing under Yosemite Lodge, above.

In the shadow of Yosemite's grand Ahwahnee, youngsters enjoy playtime in the pines.

Curry Village

YOSEMITE
NATIONAL PARK

🐾 With more than six hundred units, Curry Village comprises Yosemite's largest set of (improved) visitor accommodations. And during the summer months when all the units are full, Curry does resemble a busy little village.

Curry visitors have a choice of four types of shelter: lodge-type rooms, cabins with bath, cabins that share community bath facilities and canvas tent cabins. The tent cabins represent the park's most economic lodging.

Kids especially seem to enjoy the bustle of the village and opportunity to make new friends. There's plenty of activity to fill a day or even a week. Curry's services include cafeteria, snack shop, sports/gift shop, swimming pool, bike rentals, raft rentals and cross-country ski rentals.

From mid-November to March (weather permitting), families

flock to the Curry Village outdoor ice rink, one of the few in the western states. The rink is open during day and evening hours, and rentals are available.

During our foray onto the ice under a full winter moon, the kids spent most of the evening on their ankles and bottoms – either on the ice or around the warming fire. It's these special outings that make fond family memories.

Curry Village, Yosemite National Park, CA 95389. Reservations: telephone (209) 252-4848. Yosemite Valley is 81 miles from Merced on Highway 140. Approximately six hundred units, one hundred with private baths. Cribs and rollaways available. Pool; bike, ski and ice skating rentals. Restaurants on-site and nearby. Less expensive to moderate.

Diversions

See listing under Yosemite Lodge, above.

Wawona Hotel
YOSEMITE
NATIONAL PARK

🐾 Like the stereotypical older sibling whose good grades and athletic prowess grabbed the spotlight from the quiet one, Yosemite Valley has overshadowed Wawona for years.

Even though the Wawona Hotel is Yosemite's oldest surviving hostelry, it gets the least attention. But ask any of the guests who've been coming here for years and they'll tell you it's fine with them. The fewer who discover this gem the better.

Despite its distance from the attractions of Yosemite Valley, the area has definite family appeal. The reservations folks were responsive to our request for suitable accommodations, giving our group of four the hotel's most spacious room, behind a long, covered porch in the classic World War I–era annex.

The remaining rooms are spread among a set of quaint old

Victorian-style buildings. Several rooms have connecting doors for large families, and more than half the units have private baths.

At one end of the annex is an oak-panelled rec-type room with a TV and rock fireplace. Most folks, however, spend their time outdoors. In the midst of a huge expanse of lawn is a large swimming "tank," and the Sierra's first golf course sits adjacent to the hotel. There's also a tennis court.

Nearby is the Pioneer Yosemite History Center, where kids can explore an old jailhouse, miner's cabin and covered bridge. Seasonal demonstrations here range from soap making to spinning yarn. A stagecoach ride is also conducted by the history center. During the Christmas season, a special old-fashioned celebration is held, featuring stage rides, a lantern tour of the history center and traditional yuletime refreshments.

Wawona Hotel, Wawona, Yosemite National Park, CA 95389. Reservations: telephone (209) 252-4848. Wawona is accessible via Highway 41, about 66 miles from Fresno. Yosemite Valley is about 30 miles away. One hundred five rooms, 50 with private bath. Cribs and rollaways available. Swimming, golf and tennis. Restaurant on-site. Store nearby. Moderate.

Diversions

The park maintains riding stables at Wawona during the summer. The Mariposa Grove of giant sequoias is nearby. Ask at the desk about the Wawona Campground campfire program. The narrow-gauge Yosemite Mt. Sugar Pine Railroad runs out of Fish Camp, outside the park's boundary.

Sierra
Family Camps

❦

About Family Camps

❦ It's not exactly roughing it, and it's not exactly the Ritz. You won't have room service or someone to make your bed every morning. But neither will you have to do so much as look at a kitchen during your entire stay.

The city- and university-operated camps featured in this section offer families a chance to flee city life to enjoy a simple, laid-back week (or sometimes less) breathing mountain air, recreating and relaxing.

Locations of these camps are as diverse as Northern California's scenery—from the Lake Tahoe Basin to the area just outside Yosemite's border. While some are "closer to nature" than others (cabin electricity isn't always standard equipment at these camps), each operates on a similar schedule and plan. All are open during the summer and all are on the American plan (meals included). Accommodations are generally spartan, consisting of canvas-covered or wooden cabins with beds and mattresses. You'll share central bath and shower facilities with the other guests.

Considering what's included in the way of food and fun, rates are quite reasonable. Plan on spending at least $30 per day for each adult and somewhat less for each child. Residents of cities that sponsor camps generally get reduced rates. Current rate sheets are available year-round from reservation offices.

Thanks to cities like San Francisco and universities like Cal, summer camp isn't just for kids anymore. See you at the camp fire.

Camp Concord
SOUTH LAKE TAHOE

❦ The brochure describes Camp Concord as a "camping experience without all the inconveniences." In other words, if you're more comfortable in a bed with crisp linens and a room with maid service, you'll be happier at one of South Lake Tahoe's nearby motels. But you'd miss out on an opportunity to sample some of the unspoiled beauty of the south shore.

Camp Concord sits unobtrusively off the west-shore highway just far enough from many South Lake Tahoe attractions to make you feel you're a million miles from anything.

Run by the Bay Area city of Concord (visitors need not be residents of Concord), the facility is only a short walk from tree-lined Pope-Baldwin Beach, one of the lake's most popular beaches and the spot where camp guests often spend the better part of their Tahoe stay (although the gaming action of Stateline is only minutes away by car).

Camp Concord guests sign up for week-long stays from June through August. Accommodations are rustic but adequate, consisting of small cabins with electricity and bunks (some with double beds). Each cluster of cabins has its own "bath house" with toilets and hot showers. Guests need to bring sleeping bags and pillows.

Camp Concord is on the American plan, with three meals served daily in the camp lodge, where a welcome fire takes the bite out of the chilly Tahoe mornings.

Camp Concord, South Lake Tahoe. Reservations: 2885 Concord Boulevard, Concord, CA 94519-2698; telephone (415) 671-3273. Four-and-a-half miles north of the Highways 50 and 89 junction, turn west off Highway 89 to camp. Eighteen cabins; shared central bathroom facilities. Activities include hiking, swimming, fishing, rafting, horseback riding, volleyball and archery. Babysitting services available. Concord residents receive a discount on rates here. Three daily meals included.

Camp Sacramento

TWIN BRIDGES

🐾 Until recently, Camp Sacramento was a mystery of sorts to us. We had often whizzed by the gates on the way to South Lake Tahoe craning our necks for a glimpse of the camp through the trees.

Fortunately – for the campers – the facilities are well hidden from busy Highway 50, and one must drive down the dirt road into camp for a good look at the bustling little community.

There are 65 cabins here, each with electric lights and double and/or single beds. Neither linens nor bedding is provided, and the cabins are not equipped with running water, AC outlets or heating or air conditioning.

Camp Sacramento is geared for families, and activities are available for all ages. They include teen dances, adult/teen arts and crafts, coed volleyball, basketball, story hour, pizza night, family game night and exercise classes. Even a champagne brunch is offered. For special treats, Camp Sacramento goes the extra mile by offering barbeques and wine and cheese buffets. There are also supervised activities for young children, who are grouped according to age as "chipmunks," "minnows" and "marmots." Ping-Pong, horseshoes, baseball, video games, pool table and a well-equipped play area round out the lengthy list of things to do.

Families have a choice of week-long visits, "mini-vacations" of three days or, if accommodations are available, day visits. Reservations are required, and you don't have to be a Sacramentan to be a guest.

Camp Sacramento, Twin Bridges, CA. Reservations: Department of Parks and Community Services, 5699 South Land Park Drive, Sacramento, CA 95822; telephone (916) 449-5127. Seventeen miles southwest of South Lake Tahoe on Highway 50. Sixty-five cabins (no running water, bedding or outlets in cabins), central lavatories with showers and outlets. Three daily meals included.

The Lair of
the Golden Bear

PINECREST

🐾 Pinecrest Lake, in the Stanislaus National Forest, has been a personal favorite destination since I first attended scout camp there as a youth. It wasn't until recently, however, that we learned about the Lair of the Golden Bear, through some friends who are members of the University of California, Berkeley, Alumni Association, which operates the family camp. (The bear is Cal's mascot.)

Although the camp is operated by the alumni group, admission isn't restricted to Cal grads. The trick is to make a reservation early, as the 12 or so weekly summer sessions often fill rapidly. (Reservations are usually accepted beginning March 1.)

The Lair, staffed by amiable students from the Berkeley campus, lives up to its pledge to offer "a program for every interest." In the "Kub Korral," kids two through seven have the run of a supervised play area with swings, sand box, slide and climbing aparatus. The korral keeps the older kubs occupied with arts and crafts, cookie baking, pool games and cartoons. The two hours of supervision each morning and afternoon give parents a chance to enjoy activities like swimming in a large pool (or the nearby lake), softball, volleyball, tennis, badminton, shuffleboard, hiking or horseshoes.

Accommodations are strictly no-frills, but adequate, considering guests spend most of their time enjoying the outdoors. Semi-enclosed tent cabins with cots and mattresses (bring your own bedding) serve as sleeping quarters. Guests share modern bathroom and shower facilities.

Breakfast, lunch and dinner are served in an open-air hall. Bag lunches are available for those venturing away for the day. There's also a small store and lodge for lounging.

Since the Lair is affiliated with a major university, guests are also treated to a series of informal lectures by visiting Cal faculty and administrators.

Summer days up here range from warm to downright hot, with mornings and evenings on the cool side. Guests should bring rain gear—just in case.

The Lair of the Golden Bear, Stanislaus National Forest, Pinecrest. Reservations: Alumni House, UC Berkeley, CA 94720; telephone (415) 642-0221. Thirty miles east of Sonora. Tent cabins with cots.

Supervised programs for children and numerous activities. Three daily meals included.

Berkeley
Tuolumne Camp

GROVELAND

🐚 Add Berkeley to the list of Bay Area communities that operate family camps in the northern mountains. Berkeley's Tuolumne Camp is just a few miles up the road from San Jose's rustic summer resort near Groveland.

Tuolumne Camp is typical among family camps in terms of accommodations: floored tent-type cabins, central bath houses and family-style meals. It also offers the requisite dose of family fun: swimming, ball games, nature hikes, talent shows and planned activities for kids. The camp does have unique points, however. Most of the cabins have porches to accommodate large families and reduced rates if more than four of you share a cabin. (The porches also let campers sleep under the stars.)

While there's no need to hunt for food during your stay at Tuolumne Camp, the staff will gladly keep your catch of the day (from the local river) on ice and provide facilities for you to cook it.

There's also a camp quiet time from around 1:30 to 2:30 (a good time for naps).

Finally, the camp provides a limited number of subsidized "camperships" for low-income families, ensuring that everyone – not just those who can afford it – have a chance to enjoy a nice vacation with the family.

Berkeley Tuolumne Camp, Groveland, Tuolumne County. Reservations: City of Berkeley Camps Office, 2180 Milvia Street, Berkeley, CA 94704; telephone (415) 644-6520. Located off Highway 120 between Groveland and Yosemite. Seventy-two tent cabins with floors, porches, cots, mattresses and storage drawers. Campers bring their own bedding and pillows. Planned activities, swimming, sports, store and laundry. Berkeley residents receive reservation priority through April and a discount on rates. Three daily meals included.

San Jose
Family Camp

GROVELAND

❦ The city of San Jose jumped on the family-camp bandwagon in 1968 by establishing its own summer retreat along the middle fork of the Tuolumne River in the Stanislaus National Forest.

San Jose Family Camp enjoys an enviable central mountain location, in that there's about as much to do away from the camp as there is inside it. Yosemite National Park is only a 40-minute ride away, and historic Columbia is also within an easy drive. Other nearby attractions include Moccasin Creek Trout Hatchery and Pine Mountain Golf Course, which offers as well horseback riding and hay rides.

However, many visitors are kept busy by the numerous things to do at the camp. Programs consist of nature hikes, volleyball, softball, Ping-Pong, camp fires, skits, talent shows and arts and crafts projects. There's also a "swimmin' hole" as well as small library, nature museum, horseshoe pits, archery range, lodge, camp store and laundry facilities.

Tents with wood floors, cots and mattresses (bring your own bedding) are scattered about the camp. While the tents themselves have no electricity, outlets are provided in the community restroom/shower facilities.

Camp cooks prepare cafeteria-style breakfast and lunch at the large dining hall. Dinner is family style. Sack lunches are available on request.

Reservations are usually accepted (by mail) as early as March for sessions that run from late June through August. Guests may stay one night or longer. The camp is open to anyone, although San Jose residents get a price break.

San Jose Family Camp, Groveland, Tuolumne County. Reservations: 151 W. Mission Street, San Jose, CA 95110-1781; telephone (408) 277-4666. Located off Highway 120 east of Groveland. Tent cabins with cots and mattresses. Campers bring their own bedding and pillows. Planned activities, swimming, sports, store and laundry. Three daily meals included.

Mother Nature's "building blocks" provide a creative diversion at a Sierra family camp.

Camp Mather
RUSH CREEK

🐾 Lots of folks enjoy the mountains, but not necessarily while strapped to a backpack. Others prefer a mountain resort, but not crammed shoulder to shoulder with other nature lovers. Well, here's some good news. A Sierra vacation doesn't have to include hiking, latrines and dehydrated food. And neither does it have to mean a crowded hotel or motel complex.

What if we told you there's a place – a stone's throw from Yosemite Valley – that'll cook your meals, provide activities for your kids and keep you and a few others occupied with a swimming pool, Sierra lake and lots of places to hike? Too good to be true.

Families returning year after year grow up together at Camp Mather, one of the Sierra's best-kept secrets.

For the many families who've (quietly) been coming here for years, Camp Mather is a dream come true. Tall trees, a majestic mountain backdrop . . . the best of what this region has to offer, without the madding crowds.

My family has been visiting the Yosemite area for a long time, but it wasn't until recently that we happened to learn about Camp Mather from a San Francisco family. (The camp is operated by the San Francisco Recreation and Park Department.) Residents of the city by the bay have been keeping this place a well-guarded secret for decades. Now that the secret's out, here's a brief description of what keeps visitors coming back summer after summer.

First, the location simply can't be beat. Although Yosemite Valley is close enough for day trips, many guests just aren't interested. Situated at the rim of Tuolumne River Gorge, Camp Mather has its own little slice of heaven. The cabins are spread among lush evergreens overlooking Birch Lake near natural wonders with names like Sunrise Peak and Inspiration Point.

Planned activities for the youngsters give moms and dads a

chance to unwind, though there are lots of things to do as a family: swimming, tennis, ball games and hiking, to name a few. At night there are dances, camp fires, skits and games.

Then there's the food. While you'll undoubtedly enjoy the three hearty meals served daily, the best thing about eating at Camp Mather is that you won't have to cook or wash a single dish.

While you'll be treated like royalty in the dining hall, don't expect the accommodations to be world class. The cabins here are rustic, although a cut above the lodging provided at some other Sierra family camps. Here you'll at least have electricity. Cabins sleep up to six on beds and mattresses. Bath/shower facilities are separate.

First-time guests have little choice but to have their lodging assigned here. However, once you've become acquainted with the camp layout, the folks at Mather will let you reserve the cabin of your choice. But you'd better hurry. Chances are some other family— maybe even mine—has their eye on that same little cabin by the lake.

Camp Mather, Rush Creek, Tuolumne County. Reservations: Camp office, McLaren Lodge, Golden Gate Park, San Francisco, CA 94117; telephone (415) 558-4870. Located off Highway 120 just outside the western boundary of Yosemite National Park. Rustic cabins (with electricity) that sleep up to six on mattresses and beds. Campers bring their own bedding and pillows. Separate bath/shower facilities. Planned activities for children, swimming (lifeguard on duty) in pool and lake, ball games, tennis (bring rackets and balls), nature program, store and laundry. San Francisco residents receive discount on rates. Three daily meals included.

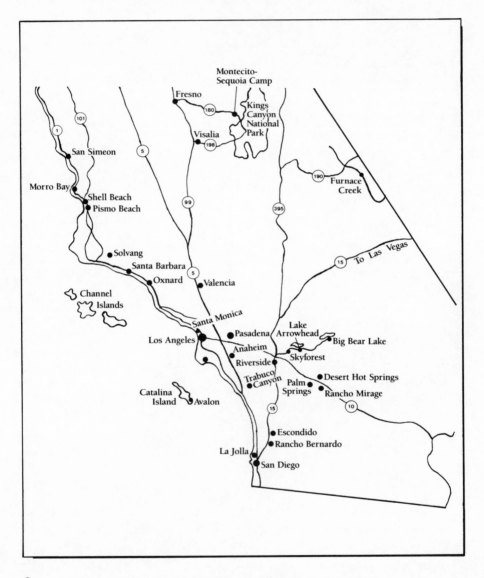

The South Coast

❦

San Simeon Pines Resort

SAN SIMEON

❦ Given the distance to Hearst Castle from California's major population centers, a visit here often means staying overnight somewhere along the road. Many families choose the San Simeon Pines Resort Motel.

This tidy nine-acre resort certainly isn't difficult to find. It sits just off scenic Highway 1 about five miles south of the castle, within a sea otter and wildlife preserve.

Intrigued by descriptions we'd heard from others who had visited the resort, we pulled off the highway to do some looking around. While the San Simeon Pines has its own nine-hole, par-three golf course, pool, shuffleboard and children's playground, we were particularly impressed with the resort's logical but rather unique arrangement of rooms. Families (we can be noisy at times) are housed in comfortable, reasonably priced rooms near the shady play area, while those traveling without children stay in a quieter area of the resort. It makes good sense to parents like us, whose offspring can often be heard around the block.

San Simeon Pines Resort Motel, Moonstone Beach Drive (P.O. Box 117), San Simeon, CA 93452. Telephone (805) 927-4648. Take

Moonstone Beach Drive off Highway 1, five miles south of Hearst Castle. Sixty rooms, pool, nine-hole golf course (short), playground, private access to Moonstone Beach. Less expensive to moderate.

Diversions

Hearst Castle is the obvious attraction in this region, but the beach here is worth a visit. San Simeon State Beach is literally across the street from the motel, via walkway. There are sea lion rocks, a rocky point with tidepools, a sandy beach with lots of polished pebbles, trails and picnic tables. This area is also a good spot from which to view migrating whales between December and April.

There's another playground at Leffingwell's Landing at the north end of Moonstone Beach Drive. The charming little village of Cambria is two miles south.

The Inn at Morro Bay

MORRO BAY

❦ A growing tourist industry has brought numerous motels and resorts to this part of the California coast in recent years. However, the Inn at Morro Bay is the central coast's only resort situated at water's edge.

Located midway between Los Angeles and San Francisco, the recently redecorated inn is a melting pot for visitors from the north and south parts of the state. Most find this area a refreshing change of pace from more celebrated getaway destinations along other parts of the coast.

The inn, which sits just beyond the shadow of hulking Morro Rock, is actually inside Morro Bay State Park, where visiting families can walk through a bird sanctuary that's home to more than 250 species. An observation area offers a look into one of the remaining blue heron rookeries.

With 10 acres of lush landscaping, the inn blends nicely with the area's natural beauty. Also worth noting is the stylish decor of the rooms. Each is individually decorated with a French country flair.

The Inn at Morro Bay is perched at water's edge near Morro Rock.

Many have fireplaces, cathedral ceilings, refrigerators, private decks and water views.

The inn's swimming and wading pools are heated year-round. Bicycles are available to guests at no charge, and golfers have access to an adjacent 18-hole course. At this writing, plans were in the works for a full-service marina, offering guest boat slips as well as canoe, kayak, fishing boat and windsurf-board rentals.

The Inn at Morro Bay, Morro Bay, CA 93442. Telephone (805) 772-5651 or, toll-free in California, (800) 321-9566. Take the Main Street exit from Highway 1. Proceed through town to the state park entrance. The resort is on the right within the park boundary. One hundred rooms and suites. Cribs available. Children stay free in parents' room. Swimming and wading pools, game room. Free use of bicycles. Moderate to expensive.

Diversions

After exploring the state park, visit the nearby Natural History Museum. Morro Bay is also home to a small aquarium, set behind the Morro Bay Gift Shop on the Embarcadero. A couple of dozen tanks hold a variety of sea creatures, from seals to eels. There's a children's playground adjacent to Morro Rock. The resort will help arrange harbor cruises aboard the *Tiger's Folly* and tickets to Hearst Castle.

Windmark Resort
SHELL BEACH

❦ Those who remember the communities of Shell Beach and Pismo Beach as quiet little burgs with quiet little motels will be surprised at some of the changes. The Windmark Resort is among the most striking.

One of the area's newest and largest resorts, the Windmark sits on a sculpted bluff overlooking the ocean, just off Highway 101. Surrounded by spindly palms and boasting a bold, contemporary style, the five-story hotel contrasts with the community's more traditional, simple architecture.

The grounds are spacious. The expanse of lawn offers lots of room for romping, and a stairway leads down to the sandy beach. Services and facilities include a swimming pool, spa, fitness center and bicycle rentals. Tennis and golf are nearby.

The resort will help guests arrange for ocean fishing trips, dune rides and tickets to Hearst Castle, which is less than an hour's drive to the north.

Windmark Resort, 2757 Shell Beach Road, Shell Beach, CA 93449. Telephone (805) 773-5000. From Highway 101 in Shell Beach, exit at Spyglass Drive and drive north on the west side of the highway to the resort. Seventy rooms and suites. Cribs and rollaways available at no charge. Children 18 and younger stay free in parents' room. Swimming pool, spa, fitness room and bike rentals. Expensive.

This area boasts a fairly consistent mild climate and is consequently a good getaway choice most any time of the year. You can't drive your car on Pismo Beach anymore, but the city has built a long pier over the ocean for strolling and fishing. The 23-mile-long, wide, sandy beach is among the state's best. There are plenty of tidepools as well. The Pismo Clam Festival is held each November. Jazz festivals bring Pismo to its feet in February and October. Monarch butterflies put on a free show every winter.

In nearby San Luis Obispo, the streets of the vintage downtown area are blocked off Thursday evenings when local farmers set up shop to sell their finest products. Street barbeques and street musicians round out the impromptu evening celebrations.

Spyglass Inn
SHELL BEACH

🐾 We've visited our share of California resorts, but the Spyglass Inn is the only one we've found that includes in its list of features an ocean-view miniature golf course. It's so dramatically placed that, if your kids put a bit too much oomph in their swing, they'll likely knock the ball over the cliff and into the ocean. The challenge may not be equal to the world-famous oceanside golf courses that dot the California coast, but putting along the bluff here with the crashing waves below is a delightful way to spend an afternoon or warm summer evening.

If you'd rather relax than golf you can keep an eye on the kids from balconies off the cliffside units facing the course. Most of the inn's rooms have panoramic views of the ocean. Suites, which offer accommodations for larger families, have private patios. All have TVs with a cable movie channel.

At the center of the complex is a fenced area holding a pool and spa. A shuffleboard deck is also provided for guests. There's a public park with playground at the end of the street if the little natives get restless.

The coastline along the inn's property is rocky, and there's no direct beach access. However, Pismo Beach's long, sandy beach is only a few minutes' drive away. A stairway behind the inn leads to a deck perched about halfway down the cliff. From here visitors have a bird's-eye view of the sometimes angry surf as it batters the coast.

Spyglass Inn, 2705 Spyglass Drive, Shell Beach, CA 93449. Telephone, toll-free, (800) 824-2612. Take the Spyglass Drive exit off Highway 101. The inn is adjacent to the west side of highway. Eighty-three rooms and suites. Cribs and rollaways available. Miniature golf on-site, pool, spa, shuffleboard, self-serve laundry, in-room cable movies. No charge for children 12 and younger. Moderate to expensive.

Diversions

See listing under the Windmark, above.

Sea Crest Resort
PISMO BEACH

❦ Among the many resorts that dot the coast just south of San Luis Obispo, the largest concentration of happy families – during our visit – was found at the Sea Crest Resort Motel.

An older establishment that has recently been modernized and expanded, the Sea Crest is a bit deceiving from the highway. The exterior facade hides the resort's real treasure. On the ocean side is a recreation area that boasts expansive lawn areas, three spas, a pool (heated year-round), shuffleboard and glass-enclosed sundeck, not to mention spectacular views of Pismo Beach and the Pacific.

Rooms at the Sea Crest are spacious and comfortable, a cut above typical motel fare. Many have ocean views. The accommodations are spread among two newer four-story complexes that flank a long, two-level unit.

Like the other establishments just north of Pismo Beach proper, the Sea Crest sits on an ocean bluff. Uncrowded, sandy beaches are only a hop, skip and jump away.

Sea Crest Resort Motel, 2241 Price Street, Pismo Beach, CA 93449.

Telephone (805) 773-4608. Take the Price Street exit from Highway 101. Motel is on the west side of the highway. One hundred sixty rooms and suites. Pool, three spas, shuffleboard and TV. Family restaurant adjacent to motel. Moderate to expensive.

Diversions

See section under the Windmark, above.

Alisal
Guest Ranch

SOLVANG

🐝 Ask the members of your family to describe their dream vacations and you'll elicit responses ranging from quiet to lively, tennis to sailing, barbeques to intimate dinners, and billiards to bingo.

Sometimes it seems that separate vacations are the only way to satisfy divergent family interests. But don't go packing everyone off in different directions just yet. Not until you look over the Alisal Guest Ranch. You'll stand a good chance of making everybody happy—and emerging as a hero.

The Alisal is to family getaways what the Hope Diamond is to jewelry. It doesn't get much better. Consider a typical day's worth of activities: breakfast horse or hay-wagon rides with lots of food and singing; supervised arts and crafts for the kids; a morning round of golf or set of tennis; a dip in the pool before lunch; a family game of horseshoes before supper; children's lakeside barbeque and a leisurely dinner for two in the ranch dining room. It's not over yet. After-dinner activities often include bingo, cartoons and family movies, square dancing, storytelling and talent shows.

With so much going on throughout the resort, most active families will spend much of the day and evening hours out and about. Yet accommodations here are comfortable and tidy enough to invite lounging in your room.

With so many family diversions at Alisal Guest Ranch, the swimming pool is rarely crowded.

Guests have a choice of studio/sitting rooms, two-room suites and three-bedroom, two-bath bungalows that resemble small homes.

The Alisal's setting can't be beat. The California ranch-style buildings are set among native oaks on acres of lawn surrounded by gently rolling hills.

Although there's a two-night minimum stay at the Alisal, the time goes by so quickly here that many families hang around a week or longer. Some have been coming since the resort opened in 1946.

Parents, many of whom vacationed here as kids, are particularly impressed with the attention focused on young visitors. Mom and dad don't have to worry about enjoying themselves. Children are not only exposed to enjoyable activities, they're in the friendly, enthusiastic hands of the counseling staff.

If you'd like to see the Alisal up close and personal before making reservations, ask the resort to mail you a copy of their 10-minute video tour. Just one suggestion. Unless you're willing to commit then and there to a visit, don't let the kids or your spouse watch the tape. Family mutinies are not a pretty picture.

Alisal Guest Ranch, 1504 Alisal Road, Solvang, CA 93463. Telephone (805) 688-6411. From Highway 101, take the Buellton exit and drive three miles to Solvang. Drive south for three miles on Alisal Road to the resort. Sixty-six rooms and cottages, all with fireplaces. Cribs and rollaways available. Pool, spa, recreation room, tennis, golf, sailing, windsurfing, horseback riding, library, planned child and adult activities, play area, babysitting services and self-serve laundry. Modified American plan (breakfast and dinner included). Expensive.

Diversions

The only reason we can imagine for leaving the resort grounds would be to visit nearby Solvang, a quaint, tourist-oriented Danish community with lots of bakeries, shops and interesting architecture.

The Vacation Center
SANTA BARBARA

🐭 Ever considered packing the family off to college for summer vacation? At the University of California, Santa Barbara, Vacation Center, you're never too old or too young.

After the university's regular session ends and the students head home for the summer, the campus is taken over by families. From late June through August, the university's alumni association operates one of Southern California's most complete camps for parents and kids. (And you don't have to be a UCSB alumnus to visit, although grads do get a price break.)

Among the most beautiful of all the state's college campuses, UCSB is set on a scenic stretch of coastal bluffs and beach. However, the safe, sandy seashore is but icing on the camp cake. Guests have access to a 75-foot-long pool, 10 tennis courts, an art museum, a library and bike trails. The list of services is likewise impressive. A comprehensive child-care program offers day-long specialized activities for kids from ages 2 through 12, as well as a teen program with local excursions and an overnight campout.

You don't have to be an alumnus to enjoy summer family fun at University of California, Santa Barbara.

If you need tennis instruction or swimming lessons, they're free here, regardless of ability levels. And if you get to feeling like a pro, you can compete in more than a dozen tournaments, from tennis to backgammon.

In addition, the camp offers craft classes, fitness programs, family entertainment (such as family carnivals, bingo and movies), seminars led by UC faculty and even adult "mixers" and wine tastings.

To get your body fueled for the myriad activities on campus, three all-you-can-eat meals a day are included in the weekly rate. (Tariffs range from around $60 for a 2-year-old to around $400 for each person over age 12.)

Accommodations consist of spacious family suites that include living room (with refrigerator), two to four bedrooms and bath. Daily maid service is provided.

A young, energetic bunch of camp staff members go out of their way to make sure you and your group reap maximum enjoyment from this Pacific paradise. This is summer school – California style.

The Vacation Center, University of California, Santa Barbara, CA 93106. Telephone (805) 961-3123. The Vacation Center is located on the campus at Goleta, just north of Santa Barbara off Highway 101. Seventy-five family suites with from two to four bedrooms each. Cribs available. Swimming pool and tennis courts (with free lessons), crafts and fitness programs, family entertainment, child care and activities (from ages two through teens). American plan (meals included). One-week minimum stay. Expensive.

El Encanto Hotel

SANTA BARBARA

❦ When vacationing with children, adults often face some tough decisions. Do you sacrifice ambience, charm and romance for a fast-paced, frenetic family resort, or do you indulge yourselves at a destination more geared to your own tastes?

When it's time to treat the grown-ups, El Encanto Hotel and Garden Villas is just the ticket. Set on a lush, sculptured hillside overlooking Santa Barbara's red-tiled roofs, El Encanto ("the enchanted") consists of 100 cottages and villas, some dating back to the early 1900's. In recent years, millions of dollars have been invested in the property in order to preserve the era when the "carriage trade" wintered here.

Since the early years of Hollywood, celebrities in search of seclusion have likewise been drawn to El Encanto's charming cottages, where privacy is the password. In fact, visiting families with infants in tow have actress (and frequent El Encanto guest) Jane Seymour to thank for a special room here. In order to accommodate Ms. Seymour and her young family, the management created a cute nursery in one of the cottages, complete with crib, changing table and rocking chair. There's even a kitchenette for preparing baby bottles. Just ask for "Jane's room" (#218).

Families with older kids might prefer adjoining rooms, a few of which are set behind quaint picket fences with private patios. Accommodations are designated as "small and cozy," "spacious and special" and "magnifique," and are priced accordingly, from $100 to around $300 per night.

Outdoor activities at El Encanto include swimming and tennis (a tennis pro is in residence), although mom and dad will probably be

Don't be surprised to see a movie star or two lounging poolside at El Encanto.

just as content enjoying simple pleasures. We became quite skilled at lounging on comfortable French country couches and chairs, strolling along red walkways that crisscross the grounds and gazing off at the ocean from a swinging outdoor love seat.

El Encanto Hotel, 1900 Lasuen Road, Santa Barbara 93103. Telephone (805) 687-5000. From Highway 101, take the Mission exit and drive to Mission Santa Barbara. Veer right onto Alameda Padre Serra, then turn left on Lasuen. One hundred cottage rooms and contemporary units, all with private bath; some with kitchenettes. Cribs available. Pool and tennis courts. Restaurant. Expensive to very expensive.

Diversions

The queen of California's missions is a half mile below the hotel. The Museum of Natural History and planetarium are a short walk away. In minutes (by car), you can be romping on the beach. The Santa Barbara Zoo, with a petting area, train ride and "Wild West playground," is on Beach Street near the ocean. A bike path follows the coast for miles, and rental shops are stationed along the route. Among the dozen or so parks in the area is Las Positas, one of the city's newest, with playgrounds, soccer fields and a fitness course. Youngsters will enjoy climbing the boulders along Mission Creek at Rocky Nook Park on Mission Canyon Road.

The Miramar

SANTA BARBARA

❦ When we happened upon the Miramar during a south-coast sojourn, we thought we'd stumbled upon quite a find. Then someone told us their family had been visiting the resort for four generations. So much for discoveries.

It's easy to understand why the Miramar has retained its popularity for so long. If there's a better spot for a year-round family-oriented resort, we haven't found it.

The Miramar occupies a tropical, 15-acre setting just south of Santa Barbara, between Highway 101 and the blue Pacific. Visitors are kept busy with numerous activities throughout the resort. The Miramar is so spread out, there are two pools. The largest of the pair, set adjacent to the frontage road, restaurant and office, appeared (on our visit) to be the most popular, probably since this part of the resort is more densely populated. A horseshoe-shaped, two-story, motel-type complex rings this pool.

If a bit more peace and quiet is what you're looking for, consider one of the blue-roofed cottages, lanai rooms or garden rooms to the north. Set among lush lawns and gardens, these rooms offer a bit more charm and privacy. The second pool serves this part of the resort.

The Miramar service and facility directory bulges, with tennis (pay-to-play), Ping-Pong, shuffleboard, play equipment, exercise rooms, sauna and spa.

Then there's the ocean. The Miramar is billed as the only Santa Barbara hotel right on the beach. From most anywhere on the grounds, the 500-foot-long stretch of private sandy beach is only a short stroll away. The resort's beach-front units command spectacular

Midday snacks at the Miramar are served in and around a real railroad car.

white-water views and are connected by a boardwalk. Beach umbrellas, back rests and mats are available here.

To access the ocean, guests pass a resort-owned rail-car-turned-diner that serves take-out fare from late morning until early evening. The beach path crosses the railroad tracks where a vintage turn-of-the-century rail station recalls days when most Miramar guests arrived by train.

Like those early California "suntan special" vacation trains, many of the Golden State's grand resorts from yesteryear have faded away. Fortunately, the Miramar has only gotten better with age.

The Miramar Hotel Resort, San Ysidro Road at Highway 101 (P.O. Box M), Santa Barbara, CA 93102. Telephone, toll-free in California, (800) 322-6983. Exit Highway 101 on the San Ysidro turnoff, three miles south of Santa Barbara. Resort is on ocean side of highway. Two hundred rooms, cottages and suites, some with kitchens. Cots and cribs available. Pools, spas, tennis, play area, Ping-Pong, shuffleboard, exercise rooms and sauna. Beach access. Two-night minimum stay Friday and Saturday; three nights on holidays. Moderate to very expensive.

Diversions

See listing under El Encanto Hotel, above.

San Ysidro Ranch

SANTA BARBARA

❦ "Our ranch," states the San Ysidro brochure, "benevolently tends the well and not-so-needy. We also spoil children."

If you're not-so-needy (or at least game for a splurge), this is a great place to unwind. You'd be in pretty famous company. Consider a few of those who have cooled their heels at the ranch. John and Jacqueline Kennedy honeymooned here. Laurence Olivier married Vivien Leigh on the grounds. Guests have also included kings and prime ministers, as well as folks like you and me.

Travelers have been bringing families here since 1893, when the ranch was a real ranch. Fruit trees scattered about the grounds serve as reminders of the early days when the hills of Montecito were lush with citrus. By the way, the ranch dining room used to be the packing shed.

Today, dozens of quaint wood and stone cottages bearing names like Magnolia, Jasmine and Tangerine dot the spacious grounds. All suites have hideabeds to accommodate extra sleepers.

The decor is luxurious, and the gardens are nicely kept. Guests' names are engraved on wooden signs that hang outside each cottage. On a hill at the north end of the resort sit a swimming pool, wading pool and tennis courts. There's also a small children's play area with some vintage equipment.

Equestrians will have a field day here. Group and private guided horseback rides are offered through miles of scenic foothill country.

The San Ysidro Ranch, and all of Santa Barbara's resorts, for that matter, are ideal choices for getaways year-round, since winter and summer temperatures vary little. Mild winter temps hover around 75 degrees.

With daily room rates ranging from about $150 "to infinity," and private cottages going from around $300, the San Ysidro Ranch is one of the most expensive resorts we visited. Boarding your horse for a night here even costs more than some modest motels charge for a room. But what other resort will treat your equine friend to "gourmet hay"?

San Ysidro Ranch, 900 San Ysidro Lane, Montecito (Santa Barbara), CA 93108. Telephone (805) 969-5046. From Highway 101, exit at San Ysidro Road and drive east for two miles. Turn right on San Ysidro Lane and follow to the ranch. Forty-three cottage rooms and suites. Cribs available. Swimming, tennis, horseback riding and children's play area. Suites have hideabeds to accommodate extra sleepers. Restaurant on-site. Expensive.

Diversions

See listing under El Encanto Hotel, above.

Casa Sirena

OXNARD

🍎 South-state families who like to blast out of Los Angeles for the weekend often look to Ventura County for solace. Casa Sirena, hidden away along Channel Islands Harbor about an hour north of L.A., is a logical destination. It's also a well-placed stopover for families headed down the coast to Southern California attractions.

One of a handful of south-state resorts owned by the Princess Cruises people, Casa Sirena is geared toward a laid-back atmosphere that encourages family fun. Rooms are spacious and comfortable, and many boast harbor views from patios or (child-resistant) balconies. Ours was equipped with a small refrigerator, which came in handy for storing family staples (juice and other snacks).

Outdoors there's a good-sized recreation area with large pool, sauna, spa, small gymnasium (grown-ups only), video games, pool tables and putting green. Tennis courts are also available, as is a stable of bikes for rides around the harbor or to a sandy beach about a mile away.

Immediately adjacent to the resort grounds is Peninsula Park, which has a nice children's playground and lots of lawn area. A walkway skirts the harbor along the park and resort for up-close viewing of the boats—and maybe even an occasional sea creature. We watched a passerby roll up his sleeves, reach into the water and pull up a big starfish from a rock along the harbor.

Casa Sirena, 3605 Peninsula Road, Oxnard, CA 93030. Telephone, toll-free, (800) 344-2626. From Highway 101, take Victoria Avenue exit south; turn right on Channel Islands Boulevard, and turn left on Peninsula Road. Two hundred seventy-three rooms and family suites, some with kitchens. Cribs and rollaways available. Pool, spa, sauna, tennis, recreation room, bike rentals and park with playground next door. Restaurant on-site. Moderate to expensive.

Diversions

Sightseeing tours of the Channel Islands, one of our newest national parks, leave this area on a regular schedule. The islands are 11 miles offshore (see the California Cruising listing in Part III of this book for details). Whale-watching excursions also are offered. Six Flags Magic Mountain (see Magic Mountain listing in Part II) is about an hour's drive east.

Catalina Island

🐭 It has a well-deserved reputation as honeymoon heaven, but Catalina Island is beginning to attract its fair share of fun-seeking families. For every dreamy-eyed couple walking hand in hand along the shore, there seems to be a family frolicking nearby.

Sitting only 22 miles west of Los Angeles, Catalina is so close—yet so far. Getting there is half the fun. An adventure in itself, a ride to the island will give the youngsters a taste of cruising on the open sea. And just when the trip begins to get boring the quaint village of Avalon, Catalina's only city, appears in the distance. The community is a breath of fresh air, figuratively and literally. There's no smog, no billboards, no car-choked boulevards and no strips lined with fast-food franchises.

Walking up an Avalon street reveals this bird's-eye view of the harbor, beach, and casino.

Thank chewing gum magnate William Wrigley for the island's slow pace and natural beauty. He bought Catalina for himself in 1919 to save it from developers. After Wrigley's death in 1977, much of Catalina was turned over to a conservancy that adopted his limited-growth philosophy.

There are only about 30 hotels in town, and tourist traffic is confined within the community of Avalon to rental vehicles.

To see the island, you'll need either a strong set of legs or a ticket for a bus tour. The tour includes performances by Arabian horses at El Rancho Escondido, refreshments at "Old Eagle's Nest" stagecoach stop and glimpses of the buffalo, goats and boar that call the island home. Other guided diversions include trail rides, glass-bottom boat rides and (from June through September) evening boat tours to see flying fish.

If you'd rather design your own Catalina adventure, there are bike rentals, boat rentals, paddleboard rentals and gentle swimming beaches. An 18-hole miniature golf course is located in Island Plaza, one block from the ocean. A regular 9-hole golf course as well as several tennis courts are also open to visitors.

The stately landmark Avalon Casino, where the big bands once played, now shows first-run movies.

Avalon, Catalina Island. For information and reservations call (213) 510-1520. Boat service is available through Catalina Express, out of San Pedro; Catalina Cruises, out of Long Beach and San Pedro; and Catalina Passenger Service, from Orange County. Advance reservations for boat transportation are advised.

Spending the Night?

The Atwater Hotel, (800) 4-AVALON, is billed as Avalon's family hotel. The Pavilion Lodge (same phone) is also a good choice. Both are operated by the Santa Catalina Island Company. The Hotel Catalina, (213) 510-0027, and Catalina Cottages, (213) 510-1010, have family cottage units. Two- and three-night minimum stays are required much of the year. Be sure to book reservations early. Avalon's one thousand rooms are usually taken months in advance. Moderate to expensive.

The Southern Mountains

❦

Montecito-Sequoia High Sierra Vacation Camp

SEQUOIA
NATIONAL FOREST

❦ As a family vacation destination, the central Sierra often takes a back seat to its northern cousins, Yosemite and Lake Tahoe. After some exploring, I'm convinced the folks who frequent this majestic region probably prefer it that way.

At the risk of incurring the wrath of the central-Sierra regulars, I'll let you in on one of their deepest secrets. It's called the Montecito-Sequoia High Sierra Vacation Camp.

Until a few years ago, I wouldn't have been allowed here. You see, for nearly 40 years it served as a retreat exclusively for girls. While programs for the female gender continue to be offered, families now compose a good portion of the guest list.

The camp enjoys a locale that embodies the best that this part of the state has to offer: world-famous sequoia forests, a high mountain lake, spectacular views and rushing streams. Add to that some man-made niceties like a swimming pool and tennis courts, along with a list of activities as long as your arm, and you've got the makings of a family resort that takes a back seat to none other.

Camp activities include the standard fare, like swimming, archery, canoeing, fishing and tennis. But the camp throws in some out-of-the-ordinary pursuits that include photo tours (there's a photo lab on site), English and western riding instruction, riflery, night swimming, floating campfires and sliding down waterfalls.

To give guests an opportunity to sample the range of activities, days are divided into four sessions: two in the morning and two after lunch. Families can recreate together or separately. There are supervised programs for infants all the way up through teens.

Despite the literally dozens of things to do, life here is never hurried. No penalties are levied for sleeping in.

There are three dozen modern lodge rooms (for up to six people) with private baths, as well as another 20 rustic cabins that share nearby bath houses. Cabin guests bring their own bedding and towels.

Sessions here generally run for one week, although shorter "mini-weeks" are offered occasionally. Vacation camp usually runs from June through Labor Day weekend.

Unlike many family camps, which remain shuttered during the off-season, the Montecito-Sequoia Lodge is transformed into a high Sierra cross-country ski center when the snow begins to fall.

Montecito-Sequoia High Sierra Vacation Camp, Sequoia National Forest. Address all correspondence to 1485 Redwood Drive, Los Altos, CA 94022. Telephone (209) 565-3388. From Fresno (65 miles), follow Highway 180 east to the Kings Canyon National Park entrance and continue one-and-a-half miles to the "Y" intersection. Turn right and drive eight miles to resort sign. Thirty-six lodge rooms with baths and 20 cabins without baths (shared facilities nearby). Cribs and rollaways available. Full range of planned activities for all ages. Instruction is offered in each. Evening social programs offered. American plan (meals included). Expensive.

Big Bear Lake
SAN BERNARDINO
NATIONAL FOREST

❦ An annual average of three hundred days of sunshine, 22 miles of gorgeous shoreline, pristine forests and all within 100 miles of Los Angeles. When it's time to get away to the mountains, Los Angelinos flock by the millions each year to Big Bear Lake.

Bringing the kids to Big Bear Lake? Don't forget shovels and buckets.

Don't let the population sign fool you. While the permanent residents number about fourteen thousand, the population swells to upwards of sixty thousand on any weekend.

During the winter months the local slopes are covered with southland skiers. Snow Valley, Southern California's largest ski area, is situated only a few miles to the east, and Goldmine, less than two miles from downtown Big Bear Lake, is a favorite among families. Nearby Snow Summit is another popular south state ski resort.

Springtime brings a whole new look to the region and signals the start of a different set of activities. Swimming isn't allowed in the lake, but water skiing and fishing (year-round) are. Visitors also keep busy roller skating at the local rink, horseback riding at Shay Meadows, cruising the lake on a tour boat, riding bikes or hopping a high-speed snowless Alpine slide after riding a quarter-mile-long chair lift to the top of a snowless ski hill. Moonridge Zoo, with its collection of native mountain critters, is open generally from Memorial Day to Labor Day.

Because the region attracts some four million visitors each year, the Chamber of Commerce has taken to advertising four routes from the L.A. Basin, including "the back way," which runs out of Victorville through Lucerne Valley.

Big Bear Lake, San Bernardino National Forest; 100 miles from the Los Angeles Civic Center. For more information, contact the Big Bear Lake Tourist and Visitor Bureau, P.O. Box 3050, Big Bear Lake, CA 92315. Telephone (714) 866-5877 or 866-4601.

Spending the Night?

Cozy Hollow Lodge, (714) 866-9694, enjoys a wooded setting on Big Bear Boulevard. This small, cozy motel has family cabins and boasts a wonderful children's play structure with elevated walkways, treehouse, swings, fireman's pole and slide that empties into a sandbox. The lodge is near the Alpine slide and horse rentals.

Lake Arrowhead Hilton Lodge

LAKE ARROWHEAD

The San Bernardino mountain resorts of Lake Arrowhead and Big Bear Lake are to south-state residents what Lake Tahoe is to Northern Californians. While Bay Area and Sacramento Valley families jockey for freeway position on Friday evenings heading for a Tahoe getaway, Los Angeles–area folks are pointing themselves in the direction of their own mountain retreats.

Lake Arrowhead, the smaller of the two bodies of water, is among Southern California's most popular year-round mountain vacation destinations. Created a century ago through an irrigation/reservoir project, Lake Arrowhead and neighboring Grass Valley Lake are currently operated by local property owners.

The area's centerpiece is Lake Arrowhead Village. Grandma and grandpa might recall the quaint village in its heyday back in the 1920's and 30's, when motion-picture stars frequently strolled the streets. The decaying buildings from that era were razed a decade ago and replaced with a modern Tyrolean-type outdoor shopping complex.

The village is also the site of Lake Arrowhead Hilton Lodge. This is a self-contained resort that accommodates families nicely. When the weather is warm, visitors can be found around the pool and two outdoor spas, on a private beach or the tennis courts or browsing the local shops; maybe even taking a cruise aboard the *Arrowhead Queen* paddlewheeler.

Indoor activities, popular during the winter months, include a fully equipped health club with an indoor running track, a game room and two indoor spas. Another plus for families is the lodge's planned program for children. Contact the activity director for details.

Lake Arrowhead Hilton Lodge, P.O. Box 1699, Lake Arrowhead, CA 92352. Telephone (714) 336-1511 or, toll-free in California, (800) 223-3307. From valley cities, take Interstate 15 to the Mountain Resorts junction (Highway 30), exit on Waterman Avenue (north) and follow it to the Lake Arrowhead sign (Highway 173). Turn left and continue two miles to stop sign. Take farthest road to left (Highway 189) and drive one-half mile to resort. Two hundred fifty-seven rooms and suites, 16 with kitchens. Cribs and rollaways available. Heated pool, four spas, two tennis courts, two racquetball courts, fitness center, game room and private beach. Restaurants on-site and nearby. Children (any age) stay free in parents' room. Expensive.

Diversions

Different seasons at Lake Arrowhead bring different festivities. For example, the Dickens Christmas Celebration offers horse-carriage rides. At Easter there's an egg hunt and in October young visitors participate in a "Halloween Haunt." Local diversions also include water-ski instruction, horseback riding, an ice skating rink (in Blue Jay) and snow skiing at Snow Valley.

The
Los Angeles Area

❦

The Queen Mary
and Spruce Goose

LONG BEACH

❦ Fifty years ago, guests aboard the *Queen Mary* were among some pretty well-to-do company. With first-class trans-Atlantic passage going for a hefty $564 back in 1936, only the most wealthy could afford a berth on the superliner.

Today, even those of us on a tight budget can afford to be a guest aboard the *Queen*. Just don't expect to leave port.

Permanently berthed in Long Beach (on the Pacific) for the past several years, the floating landmark, considered the most luxurious ocean liner ever to sail the seas, has been converted into one of California's most famous hotels. It's also a growing tourist attraction, having added to its sprawling complex Howard Hughes' giant seaplane the *Spruce Goose*, a replica of an English shopping village and, more recently, a 3-D movie theater.

Families who venture aboard the *Queen Mary* to spend a night have a chance to soak up some of the extravagance that was once the exclusive domain of the world's upper crust. The 390 staterooms aren't your run-of-the-mill, cramped cruise-ship quarters. They're the largest ever built on a ship.

The decor is original, down to portholes, panelled walls and

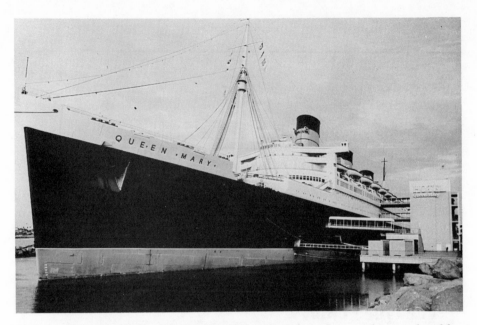

Overnight guests who board the Queen Mary *for a night sample Old World splendor without a trans-Atlantic tariff.*

period furnishings. The plumbing is contemporary, but the bathtubs feature spigots that once served up hot and cold fresh water or hot and cold salt water from the ocean.

The public areas have likewise been preserved. The Observation Bar is a striking Art Deco affair, and the Grand Salon is the setting for Sunday brunches. Picadilly Circus, the ship's original shopping mall for first-class passengers, holds such shops as the Queen Mary's Doll House, which sells unusual children's toys and gifts.

The *Queen Mary* "shipwalk" tour gives visitors a chance to poke around the myriad nooks and crannies of the thousand-foot-long ship. Included in the self-guided tour are the engine room, a film depicting the ship's origins, World War II displays (the *Queen* once served a stint as a troop carrier), captain's quarters and various decks. Personalized smaller group tours of behind-the-scenes areas are available for an extra charge.

That huge aluminum dome adjacent to the ship houses the *Spruce Goose*, the legendary flying boat constructed by Howard Hughes during the 1940's. Visitors actually board the craft – the largest airplane ever built – and peer into the flight deck and giant cargo bay. A 3-D motion picture is shown here as well.

Also on the grounds is Londontowne Village, fashioned after a 19th-century English shopping village. The complex includes boutiques and snack shops offering English wares. After all, mate, a trip to the *Queen Mary* wouldn't be complete without fish and chips.

The *Queen Mary* and *Spruce Goose*, 1126 Queensway Drive (mailing address: P.O. Box 8), Long Beach, CA 90801. Telephone (213) 435-3511. From Interstate 5, take the Long Beach Freeway (south). Follow signs to the *Queen Mary.* Three hundred ninety staterooms and suites. Cribs and rollaways available. Shops and restaurants onboard. Live shows held during summer months. Room rates include admission to shipwalk tour and *Spruce Goose* attractions. Children under 12 stay free in parents' room. Moderate to expensive. (Nonhotel visitors pay for access to the individual ship and *Spruce Goose* attractions.)

Disneyland Hotel

ANAHEIM

As we stepped off the airport bus and walked through the vast hotel courtyard surrounded by waterfalls, pedalboats, a tropical beach and miniature race cars, our wide-eyed four-year-old exclaimed, "Wow, Disneyland is great!"

Through the eyes of one so young, the confusion is understandable, given the hotel's myriad activities and facilities. If Disneyland had been closed during our visit, I'm convinced our kids probably wouldn't have been too disappointed – as long as we were staying at the park's namesake hotel.

When I stayed here as a youth during the early 1960's, the hotel had just opened its Sierra Tower, the first high-rise in Orange County. My how things have changed! Today the resort takes in three soaring towers, a dizzying array of shops and restaurants, an expansive inland "marina," a tennis club, three swimming pools, a palm-lined beach and a waterfront playland.

Our room in the Bonita Tower was spacious and comfortable. A small, in-room refrigerator came in handy for holding juice and milk. Outside, a maze of walkways and stairs invited exploration of koi ponds, Oriental gardens, streams and a cascading waterfall.

At the waterfront playland, kids maneuver coin-operated miniature tugs around a harbor dominated by a hulking replica of the *Queen Mary*. Little ones are also attracted to a racetrack with remote-controlled cars. Pedalboats are available for rent here as well.

In addition, the resort stages various entertainment programs. During our visit, shows ranged from a puppet theater to a summer Polynesian musical.

The hotel has no shortage of clean, family-oriented restaurants with children's menus. During the summer months, kids can mingle with one of Mickey Mouse's friends at a "character breakfast" offered at one of the hotel's restaurants.

Adult guests who enjoy getting away by themselves have come to the right place. In order to give mom and dad an opportunity to enjoy some of the adult-oriented entertainment (there are more than a dozen restaurants and lounges), the hotel offers supervised children's programs. The "Yukon Klem Klub," which meets during the summer and special holidays, is an evening program for ages 5 to 12 that includes dinner, games, skits and arts and crafts projects. The sessions are led by activity counselors.

A daily program of free supervised recreation activities is also held during the summer and holidays. Young guests enjoy pool-side bingo, a treasure hunt and sand-castle-building contests.

For hassle-free access between hotel and park, the Disneyland Hotel has no rival. The monorail system shoots guests directly into Tomorrowland, and an open-air tram makes regular runs to the main ticket-booth area.

Anyone who has ever visited Anaheim knows there are more accommodations surrounding Disneyland than Campbell's has soups. However, during previous trips to the park, returning to one of the anonymous local motels after an exciting day at Disneyland was always somewhat of a letdown. As guests of the Disneyland Hotel, however, we actually found ourselves looking forward to getting back to our room and exploring the grounds.

Finally, a word to the wise. Be certain to book your stay here well in advance, especially if you're planning a summer visit. We waited almost too long to make our reservation. And with two youngsters hanging their summer dreams on that trip, the family consequences, had I lost out, would have been brutal.

Disneyland Hotel, 1150 West Cerritos Avenue, Anaheim, CA 92802. Telephone, toll-free, (800) 854-6165. From Interstate 5 or 57, take the Katella Avenue exit (west). From Katella, turn right on West Street and continue to the hotel. Twelve hundred rooms and suites, some with refrigerators and wet bars. (Free Disney TV channel in all rooms.) Cribs available. Three swimming and wading pools, tennis complex (10 courts), family entertainment, supervised children's programs during summer and holiday periods, free tram transportation to and from the park, shopping complex, 16 restaurants and lounges. Children 18 and younger stay free in their parents' room. Expensive.

Coto de Caza

TRABUCO CANYON

❦ The area around Trabuco Canyon, desolate countryside only a few years ago, is undergoing an incredible transformation. During our drive up to Coto de Caza, new developments were going up everywhere. Tractors were busy carving out roads, shopping centers were rising from the fields, and skeletons of new homes and apartments stretched for miles. On the outskirts of all this sits Coto de Caza, a 4,000-acre planned development whose pricey estates would rival almost any in California.

To complement the new community, developers built Club de Caza, designed not only for local dues-paying members but for those of us interested in a visit to the resort. Guests stay in 100 modern units clustered near a posh recreation center.

Facilities include two pools (one's for kids), racquetball courts, basketball, volleyball, bowling, billiards, golf course (designed by Robert Trent Jones), exercise room and rental bikes. Nearby is the resort's equestrian center, which hosted part of the 1984 Olympic Games.

At the time of our visit, Coto de Caza was offering a nice perk: a no-cost supervised summer youth program for children (ages 5 to 12) of resort guests.

Coto de Caza, One Coto de Caza Drive, Coto de Caza, CA 92679. Telephone (714) 858-1500. From Interstate 5, take the El Toro Road (north) exit. Turn right on Santa Margarita Parkway and follow it to the resort. Coto de Caza is 30 minutes south of the John Wayne

Orange County Airport. One hundred rooms and suites, some with kitchens. Cribs and rollaways available. Swimming pools, racquetball, bowling, billiards, volleyball, basketball, tennis college, golf course, equestrian center and bike rentals. General store and restaurant. Moderate to expensive.

The Desert

❦

Furnace Creek Ranch

DEATH VALLEY

❦ The drive to Death Valley has to rank as one of the all-time greatest tests of a young child's patience. After hundreds of dusty miles (about three hundred from Los Angeles) and probably as many "Are we there yets?," the sight of Furnace Creek Ranch will be a most welcome one.

An oasis in the purest sense of the word, Furnace Creek Ranch has made this forbidding region quite palatable. Although there's plenty around to remind you that you're in the middle of a desert, the grounds are verdant, hundreds of date palms crowning the resort with plumes of green.

The ranch is actually one of two sprawling complexes here, both run by the same company. Next door is Furnace Creek Inn, the smaller, stately, Spanish-style hostelry that sits terraced against the foothills of the Funeral Mountains.

The inn, while not stuffy or pretentious, is the more formal of the two. Male guests are requested to wear a jacket to the main dining room and supper club, and the prices are a bit higher since lodging is on the American Plan (meals included). The atmosphere at the ranch is less structured and more casual. Instead of a supper club there's a cafeteria with an à la carte menu, a coffee shop and steak house. No dress code here.

Desert horseback tours conjure up images of Death Valley's famous twenty-mule teams.

While the inn is open only from November to April, the ranch welcomes guests year-round. Accommodations at the ranch range from deluxe rooms facing the golf course or swimming pool to rustic cabins that families should find particularly appealing. All rooms and cabins are air conditioned, by the way. While the year-round average temperature is a comfy 77 degrees, the mercury can climb well above the century mark during the summer months.

A desert vacation, while at times on the warm side, doesn't necessarily mean sitting in the sand watching cacti grow. The ranch offers a solid list of recreational facilities and activities that families can enjoy together.

One of the nicest features is the ranch pool, whose constant 84-degree water is supplied by a mountain spring. There's also horseback riding, golf, tennis (on lighted courts), shuffleboard, badminton, basketball, Ping-Pong and volleyball. You can also hike among the Walking Hills Sand Dunes or into Gold Canyon, or hop a rental bike and pedal to the historical Harmony Borax Works. Swings, slide and a merry-go-round are part of a playground park area at the resort.

The kids will be too young to remember TV's popular "Death Valley Days" or the sponsor's presidential pitch man, but they'll enjoy the Visitor Center and museum that recall those early years of the valley.

Furnace Creek Ranch, Death Valley, CA 92328. Telephone (619) 786-2345. The resort is situated in Death Valley National Monument about 300 miles northeast of Los Angeles, 525 miles southeast of San Francisco and 140 miles northwest of Las Vegas. Two hundred twenty-five poolside and fairway rooms and cabins. Cribs and roll-aways available. Pool, golf, tennis, bike rental, horseback riding, playground/park area, shuffleboard, game room, badminton, volleyball, basketball, Ping-Pong, weekly bingo, movies and nightly park service programs. Three restaurants, gift shops, general store and museum. Moderate (reduced rates in summer).

Rancho
Las Palmas Resort
RANCHO MIRAGE

🐭 I must admit that, on my few trips to the Palm Springs area, adults seemed to greatly outnumber kids at the resorts we visited. It's somewhat of a mystery, given the number of well-equipped resorts, the ample activities that families can enjoy together and the area's proximity to Los Angeles (two hours by car).

True, many of the resorts and businesses here cater to the terminally trendy or retired set. But we found a few that try hard to make kids feel at home.

Rancho Las Palmas is a good example. The Marriott Corporation reclaimed some 27 acres of desert and turned them into a lush wonderland of lakes, fairways (27 holes), pools (3) and tennis courts (25 of them). There's also a fitness center, as well as in-room TV movies and laundry facilities. For small ones, the grounds include a wading pool, jungle gym, swings and a picnic area. Located in Rancho

The lush grounds of Rancho las Palmas are expansive enough to explore on two wheels.

Mirage a short drive from Palm Springs, Rancho Las Palmas has more than 450 modern rooms, each with either a patio or balcony. Many face the golf course.

You might have guessed there's a price to pay for luxuriating at this desert oasis. Rancho Las Palmas is one of the more expensive resorts we've visited, with rooms going for well over $200 per night during peak season (December through May). If it's any consolation, there's no extra charge for kids under 10 years.

They obviously call this the playground of the rich and famous for good reason. Say, maybe I finally figured out why we haven't seen many families in Palm Springs.

Rancho Las Palmas Resort, 41000 Bob Hope Drive, Rancho Mirage, CA 92270. Telephone (619) 568-2727. From Highway 10, take the Bob Hope/Ramon Road exit and drive four miles to the resort. Four hundred fifty-six rooms and suites. Cribs and rollaways available. Pools, spas, 25 tennis courts, golf courses, fitness center and children's play area. Restaurants on-site. Expensive (reduced rates in summer and fall).

Diversions

See listing under Desert Princess, below.

Desert Princess

PALM SPRINGS

🐦 In an area with literally hundreds of hotels, motels and resorts, the Desert Princess is a shining star. Although it's one of Palm Springs' most recent additions, the resort is already earning a first-rate reputation. Operated by Princess Cruises Resorts (the "Love Boat" people), the Desert Princess spans nearly 350 acres on the edge of the city, surrounded by desert and upscale residential developments.

The 300 rooms are all elegantly furnished, with built-in refrigerators, remote-control TV, cable movie channel, built-in hair dryers and individual safes. We were lucky enough to get a room facing the pool, golf course and city, with the San Jacinto Mountains providing a scenic backdrop and setting off a beautiful sunset. All rooms have balconies or terraces. For those seeking more space and privacy, the Desert Princess rents one-, two- or three-bedroom condos on the lush grounds.

Recreation opportunities here are plentiful, and include an 18-hole golf course, 10 all-weather tennis courts (5 are lighted), 2 racquetball courts, 2 spas, saunas, jogging trails and a large, heated swimming pool. Bike rentals are also available.

While children of all ages are welcome, my wife and I agreed the Desert Princess and its activities and restaurants are best suited for families with older kids – or extremely well-mannered young ones. The thought of our little guys careening down the nicely carpeted halls dodging objets d'art conjured terror.

Desert Princess, Vista Chino at Landau (mailing address: P.O. Box 1644), Palm Springs, CA 92263. Telephone, toll-free, (800) 344-2626 for reservations. Three hundred rooms and suites. Pool, golf, tennis, racquetball, health club, bike rentals and jogging trails. Expensive.

Swim suits, tennis togs, and golf garb are the uniforms-of-the-day at the Desert Princess.

Diversions

The Palm Springs Aerial Tramway is one of Southern California's best skyrides. A 15-minute (fast) ascent up the granite face of Mount San Jacinto takes riders past five separate climate zones, from Sonoran Desert to Arctic/Alpine. Before we left our hotel we were swimming in the pool; a half-hour later at the top of the tram we were throwing snowballs. There are mule rides at the top. The Palm Springs Desert Museum downtown has a series of interesting, changing exhibits about the desert.

Desert Hot Springs
Hotel and Spa

❦ A visit to Desert Hot Springs Hotel and Spa is like a meal under the "Golden Arches." You get an honest deal and change back.

With rates about half what many of the area's luxury resorts charge, this place is one of the desert's best bargains. Don't expect ritzy accommodations. The hotel isn't fancy, but the rooms were clean and the guests were enjoying themselves during our visit.

The resort's main attraction is its hot, natural (and odorless) mineral water served up in seven pools and spas, including a wading pool. The hotel pumps the water from 200 feet underground directly into the pools as well as into guest rooms for drinking and bathing.

Because rooms are situated at the edge of the pool patio/courtyard, second-floor accommodations afford the most privacy. You'll also save a few dollars by staying on the second floor.

In addition to a refreshing dip in the pools, guests can also get (for an extra charge) a therapeutic massage or "European facial," or rent a poolside cabana.

The pools, saunas and decks are available on a day-use basis for those staying elsewhere. The resort sits on the uphill edge of Desert Hot Springs, a small, nondescript town at an elevation about twelve hundred feet above the desert floor. Palm Springs is a 15-minute drive away.

Desert Hot Springs Hotel and Spa, 10805 Palm Drive, Desert Hot Springs, CA 92240. Telephone (619) 329-6495. Five miles north of Interstate 10 interchange with Palm Drive. Fifty rooms. Cribs and rollaways available. Mineral pools, wading pools and spas. Less expensive to expensive.

Diversions

See listing under Desert Princess, above.

The
San Diego Area

❧

Rancho Bernardo Inn

RANCHO BERNARDO

❧ Initial impressions can be deceiving. At first glance, the Rancho Bernardo Inn had the trappings of those terminally trendy destinations favored by the well-heeled whose noses point skyward. (Our rental Ford was conspicuous among a parking lot full of Mercedes and BMWs.)

But by the time we had strolled the grounds and enjoyed a swim, those superficial airs had worn off. The inn is a casually elegant place run by friendly folks who encourage informality and fun, regardless of the make of your car.

Although many California resorts offer the type of activities available here, the Rancho Bernardo Inn seems to go one step further. Instead of one pool, there are two, as well as spas. Tennis anyone? This place has 12 courts—and a tennis college. And as if one golf course weren't enough, the Rancho Bernardo Inn operates two. Hungry? There are two restaurants to choose from: a more formal dining room and a casual one with an outdoor setting.

The inn also goes the extra mile in the care and feeding of guests. Realizing that mom and dad enjoy an occasional opportunity to pursue activities independent of their youngsters (and vice versa), the inn offers a children's camp. Normally held in August (as well as during Christmas and Easter vacation periods), the program is for ages 4 to 17. Kids spend their day and evening at camp doing arts and crafts, swimming, playing miniature golf, watching movies, playing such games as earth ball and flying-disc golf and making ice cream. Activities are geared to specific ages.

When it's time to call it a day, guests retreat to red-tile-roofed haciendas situated along the golf course and amid rolling garden settings. The 236 rooms and suites are comfortable, with a decor that can probably best be described as California ranch.

Our room was so pleasant that we opted for eating in. Although our son's favorite wasn't on the menu, room service here specializes in whipping up such dishes from scratch. Within a few minutes of placing the order, the little one was sipping the best chicken-noodle soup he'd ever tasted. He wanted more for breakfast the next morning.

Rancho Bernardo Inn, 17550 Bernardo Oaks Drive, San Diego, CA 92128. Telephone (619) 487-1611. From Interstate 15 at Rancho Bernardo (just south of Escondido), take the Rancho Bernardo Road exit, and drive east to Bernardo Oaks Drive (at the third traffic light). Turn left and drive 1 mile to the resort. The inn is about 30 miles from downtown San Diego and about two-and-a-half hours from Los Angeles. It's also close to the San Diego Zoo's Wild Animal Park. Two hundred thirty-six rooms and suites. Cribs available. Supervised children's programs during selected summer months and during Christmas and Easter holidays. Two swimming pools, spas, tennis college and two golf courses. Two restaurants. Expensive.

San Diego Princess

SAN DIEGO

🐭 Former guests might remember this rambling San Diego resort by the sea as Vacation Village. However, with the purchase of the property a few years ago by Princess Cruise Resorts, Vacation Village became the San Diego Princess.

Fortunately, some things never change. It's still very much a village of vacationers. During our brief stay, "villagers" were frolicking on the beach, playing in the pools, boating on the bay and peddling four-wheeled cycles around the lush grounds.

One of the south state's more unusual-looking coastal resorts, the Princess consists of about 450 flat-topped villas situated along Mission Bay or clustered among tropical garden settings near the water. The dwellings are connected by a maze of narrow lanes that snake through the grounds.

Our bay suite, equipped like a home away from home, featured a small kitchen, serve-yourself bar, living room, bedroom, spacious closets, and an outdoor patio facing a gentle swimming beach. Daytime views of beachcombers and small boats transformed into a dazzling display of city lights at night.

Since the beach was about five steps from the door, our family was content to stay close to home. But for those seeking a bit more activity, there's plenty to do. A bike shop rents all types of cycles, from coaster scooters to bicycles built for two. With five swimming pools and the bay, access to water is never very far away, regardless of your room's location. For tennis buffs, there are eight courts. There's also a tower whose enticing lookout affords a bird's-eye view of the grounds and surrounding area. (A safety railing on top protects even the smallest of kids.)

At meal time, guests can either hit the town (Old Town restaurants are only a short drive away) or dine at one of three restaurants on the grounds. There are plenty of scenic walkways and foot bridges for after-dinner strolls.

My family had only one complaint about the San Diego Princess. They didn't get to stay long enough. Unfortunately, spending a single night next to the beach along the gentle bay was just enough to make them (and me) want more.

San Diego Princess, 1404 West Vacation Road, San Diego, CA 92109. Telephone (619) 274-4630. From Interstate 5, take the Sea World Drive exit and drive west (past Sea World) to Ingraham. Turn right and continue to the resort (on left). Four hundred fifty rooms and suites, many with kitchens. Cribs and rollaways available. Five swimming pools, eight tennis courts, swimming beach, boat and bike rentals. Three restaurants. Expensive.

Diversions

Considering all the charm and friendly small-town atmosphere of San Diego, it's hard to believe it is our state's second largest city. It's also among the best destinations for a California family getaway, as evidenced by the number of full-service resorts. When you're not lounging around the beach or pool, there's much to see in town. Balboa Park—all one thousand acres of it—is a family favorite. The museums here are definitely worth a visit. The Aerospace Museum at Pan America Plaza houses space vehicles, historic airplanes and other aerial exhibits. The Maritime Museum on North Harbor Drive consists of three historic ships: the *Star of India* sailing ship, a ferryboat and a turn-of-the-century steam-powered yacht. Old Town is the city's historic section, where restored buildings recall the early days. Lots of shops here. And if you're game for more shopping, head out West Harbor Drive to Seaport Village, where you'll find more than 80 specialty stores as well as an old carousel to entertain the kids.

Kona Kai Beach and Tennis Resort

SAN DIEGO

🐾 Shelter Island, home of the venerable Kona Kai Beach and Tennis Resort, is that skinny slip of land that on a map looks like a side view of a skeleton's foot sitting in San Diego Bay. It also sits almost entirely surrounded by military establishments. To the north, on the other side of the bay, are Camp Nimitz, an antisubmarine warfare school, the Marine Corps recruit depot and a Coast Guard air station. To the south is a sprawling military reservation, and on the east is the huge U.S. Naval Air Station. Rest assured you'll be well protected while vacationing on Shelter Island.

Despite its skimpy size, the island is home to an assortment of old and new hotels, motels and restaurants. One of the originals, the Kona Kai once hosted many of the greats of tennis and the entertainment world. Stars like comedian Jerry Lewis used to spend summer vacations here with their families, and celebrity tournaments attracted some of the biggest names in tennis.

These days, you're likely to be surrounded by just plain folks, lured by sun, sand and recreation. The attractions of San Diego may be tempting, but you might never get around to leaving the island.

The resort offers enough of its own pastimes to keep even the most active families busy for days.

Boats and canoes are available for rent on the private San Diego Bay beach. There are wading and swimming pools, a children's beach playground, health spa with aerobic classes and weight-training facilities, tennis and racquetball courts, volleyball, basketball and bicycling.

Accommodations at the Kona Kai, starting at over $100 per night, range from beach lanais to two-bedroom suites. Most offer panoramic bay views.

Recent innovations have brought the Kona Kai many contemporary touches, but there are still nostalgic reminders of what the resort must have looked like in its earlier years, back when "Tiki lamps" and Polynesian decor were all the rage. The Kona Kai is a survivor just waiting to be rediscovered.

Kona Kai Beach and Tennis Resort, 1551 Shelter Island Drive, San Diego, CA 92106. Telephone, toll-free in California, (800) 231-9589. From Interstate 5, take the Rosecrans exit and drive two-and-a-half miles to Shelter Island Drive. Turn left and drive to the resort at the end of the island. One hundred sixty-five rooms and suites, 40 with kitchens. Cribs and rollaways available. Swimming pools, gentle beach, children's playground, tennis, racquetball, volleyball, basketball, health club and bike and boat rentals. Restaurant. Expensive.

Diversions

See listing under San Diego Princess, above.

Hilton Beach and Tennis Resort
SAN DIEGO

❧ In a city that's not the easiest to navigate, the Hilton Beach and Tennis Resort is one of San Diego's most easily accessible destinations. Motorists using Interstate 5 can't miss the sprawling resort, situated just off a particularly scenic stretch of freeway.

From the road, this could pass for just another imposing hotel. However, those who opt for a closer look are treated to a pleasant surprise. Behind the rather plain facade is a veritable garden paradise with swaying palms, lush lawn areas, large pool and a generous stretch of beach.

Set against Mission Bay, the Hilton resort is a logical choice for families looking for fun in the sun and relaxation, as well as for those seeking a central home base from which to explore San Diego.

If your plans do call for some serious local wandering, make sure to allow time to enjoy what the resort has to offer. There are two pools, putting greens, boat rentals, health club, video games adjacent to the main pool and a fenced-in children's play area.

A paved jogging/bicycle path skirts the grounds and runs along the swimming beach, and you can rent various types of bikes at a little shack nearby. Although a thick cover of clouds hid the sun during my visit to the resort, a number of families were biking, jogging and skating along the scenic path. A popular destination is the large public park and playground just down the beach.

If venturing out into the water in style sounds intriguing (it's certainly not inexpensive), you've come to the right place. The resort has a 47-foot-long yacht called *Lady Hilton* ready and waiting.

Hilton Beach and Tennis Resort, 1775 East Mission Bay Drive, San Diego, CA 92109. Telephone (619) 276-4010. From Interstate 5, take the Clairmont Mesa exit and drive one mile south on East Mission Bay Drive to the resort. Three hundred fifty-four rooms, suites and lanais, all with private balconies or terraces. Cribs and rollaways and self-serve laundry available. Two pools, five tennis courts, health club, volley ball, shuffleboard, putting greens, children's play area, boat rentals and (coin-operated) game room. Three restaurants. Expensive.

Diversions

See listing under San Diego Princess, above.

La Jolla Beach and Tennis Club

LA JOLLA

❦ In previous excursions through La Jolla, we somehow missed this "family jewel." We were finally tipped off by a young mom who fondly recalled spending summer family vacations here as a girl.

La Jolla Beach and Tennis Club is situated just up the coast from bustling La Jolla village, which bears the brunt of the tourist traffic. Only the resort's distinctive red-tiled roofline and brightly colored beach umbrellas are visible from "downtown" La Jolla.

Guests who are able to navigate the residential streets that lead to the club are greeted (after passing through a guarded entry) by rows of spindly palms framing a nine-hole pitch-and-putt course. Once past the guard house, the lane winds past a tropical lagoon to the rambling, chocolate-colored apartment complexes that face the Pacific.

Many of the 76 apartments and 15 rooms face the ocean. Apartment units are set up for "housekeeping," and all have televisions.

Although this is actually a private club, guests have full use of a private beach, fresh-water pool heated year-round, a dozen tennis courts, beach furniture and umbrellas, Ping-Pong, croquet and massage services. There are 3 restaurants on-site, and a dance band performs during the evening (if you can get a sitter for the kids).

During our brief visit a summer fog was hiding the sun, but that didn't stop many young guests from romping along and digging in the sandy beach. With one of the area's best bathing beaches, this resort offers a safe seaside environment for young children. The older and more adventurous members of your group might want to trade their water wings for a surfboard and catch some La Jolla waves with the locals. There's something for everyone here.

La Jolla Beach and Tennis Club Apartments, 2000 Spindrift Drive, La Jolla, CA 92037. Telephone (619) 454-7126. From southbound Interstate 5, take La Jolla Village Drive (west). Turn left at Torrey Pines Road, right on La Jolla Shores Drive and left to the resort. From northbound Interstate 5, take the Ardath Road exit. Turn right on La Jolla Shores Drive and left into the resort. Ninety-one rooms and apartments, many with kitchens. Private beach, pool, pitch-and-putt golf course, 12 tennis courts, 3 restaurants, self-serve laundry and daily maid service. Moderate to expensive.

II

Theme Parks
and
Big Time Fun

🐭 California's love affair with the amusement park began before the turn of the century, when our great-grandparents braved roller coasters at oceanside fun spots like San Francisco's Playland and the Santa Monica Pier.

While only fond memories remain of many of those early parks, others have not only taken their places but broadened their appeal. California is home to the nation's oldest theme park, the world's best-smelling and most colorful parade, Walt Disney's first park and the finest wild animal park this side of Africa.

From thrill rides to elephant rides, the Golden State has enough major amusement and theme parks to keep your family smiling for a month of Sundays.

Northern
California

❦

Wine Touring
with Children

❦ The fact that you're visiting with the kids doesn't mean you have to avoid the winery trails. Granted, children will likely grow weary visiting winery after winery. Seeing more than one wine press or storage tank will probably set off a chorus of "Not another winery!"

When winery touring with the younger set, the trick is to find an establishment that not only welcomes kids but offers something that'll grab their short attention spans. While children will find some wineries about as interesting as a museum of antique buttons, we found a few establishments where the kids seemed, if not to be having a rip-roaring time, at least intrigued by the facilities and grounds. After combing dozens of wineries (a tough job, but someone had to do it), we narrowed our list to the following.

The caves and passageways of Buena Vista Winery make it a favorite among adventurous visitors of all ages.

Stevenot Winery
2690 San Domingo Road, Murphys

After a visit to Mercer Cavern outside the Mother Lode burg of Murphys, drive up the road a couple of miles farther and visit Stevenot Winery. The tasting room here is an old log-walled, sod-roofed cellar of sorts. Ask the proprietors to tell you about the American Indian ghost legend and about the criminal who once called the cellar his home. The kids will be wide-eyed.

Buena Vista Winery
18000 Old Winery Road, Sonoma

This is a classic old stone winery whose tunnels are carved into a limestone hill. One of the attractions here is the self-guided tour, allowing families to move at their own speed. Children will enjoy exploring the dimly lit tunnels. Auto traffic is restricted on the grounds, so there's no worry about letting the kids roam about. There are shaded tables for picnics here, as well.

Chateau Montelena
1429 Tubbs Lane, Calistoga

The enchanting stone facade of this fine, century-old winery is right out of a fairy tale. The adjacent grounds, however, are reminiscent of a Chinese garden. You'll need a reservation to explore or picnic here, but it's worth the effort. There are graceful footbridges, a small lake, colorful tea houses and even an old Chinese junk. This is one of Napa Valley's best-kept secrets.

Sterling Vineyards
1111 Dunaweal Lane, Calistoga

The locals call this winery "Disneyland North." It's definitely designed for tourists, and children love it. You're transported from the valley floor to the winery via aerial tram, high above the treetops to the top of the hill. Kids 16 and under ride for free.

The winery is large, and tours are self-guiding. Many of the observation areas are elevated, but the formidable safety rail, while there to protect, will obscure the view of very small ones. Chances are, however, the children will be more interested in climbing stairs and exploring the many hallways than in looking at vats and presses.

Marine World
Africa USA

VALLEJO

🐭 Growing up in Northern California during the 1950's, the closest I ever got to a dancing dolphin was watching

"Flipper" on TV. And seeing a tiger jump through a flaming hoop was out of the question, unless a circus happened to breeze through our town.

Today, at Marine World Africa USA, youngsters can get close to graceful water mammals that would turn Flipper green with envy, and wild animals that put most traveling circuses to shame.

This theme park, which began simply as Marine World in the late 1960's, moved from its original home south of San Francisco to Vallejo in 1986. We had heard favorable reports from parents about the "new" park. And, in fact, judging from the virtual absence of whines and the intensity of the snores during the ride home, a day trip to this park was considerably more fun than our kids are used to.

The decision to get an early start proved a wise strategy. Lines to the park's shows were manageable in the early morning but grew longer and longer during the day. (And standing in a long line with an active four-year-old is about as much fun as being nibbled by ducks.)

Rather than rushing around aimlessly, we took some time just beyond the entrance to study the daily schedule of shows and map out a loose itinerary. Forging ahead without a basic plan will likely result in mad dashes back and forth across the 65-acre park in a tiring attempt to see it all.

By taking into consideration the various showtimes and distances between attractions, you'll have no problem enjoying all the park has to offer. And there is much to see and do here. Shows include performing killer whales, dolphins and sea lions; a water-ski extravaganza; jungle theater; exotic and predatory birds; and "Ecology Theater."

Elsewhere there's an innovative playground for kids aged 3 to 12, and a "gentle jungle" with an animal petting area and a subterranean prairie-dog town where children can come face to face with the critters. Elephant and camel rides are also offered.

For show-bound families, here are a few tips. The first few rows at the whale and dolphin show are in a splash zone, and we watched lots of folks get thoroughly drenched by the hulking whales. On the other hand, the seats toward the top of the large grandstand don't give the small kids a true appreciation of the size of these creatures. Midway is the best bet.

At the "Ecology Theater" try to sit as close to the action as possible, since some of the animals are small. For the best show seating throughout the park, arrive early. In spite of the ample bench space,

Don't sit in the first few rows during Marine World's whale show unless you've brought along a change of clothes.

animals often perform before standing-room-only crowds. And the shows always start on time.

A final hint. Bay Area weather is notoriously fickle, so dress in layers and peel down as the fog rolls out to make way for the sun. And depending on how close the kids want to get to a jumping whale, taking a change of clothes wouldn't be a bad idea.

Marine World Africa USA, Marine World Parkway, Vallejo, CA 94589. Telephone (707) 643-ORCA. About 30 miles east of San Francisco, exit east off Interstate 80 at Marine World Parkway, and turn left on Fairgrounds Drive. Ages three and under are free.

Spending the Night?

In Vallejo, try the Best Western Royal Bay Inn (with pool), 44 Admiral Callaghan Lane (moderate) or the Gateway Motor Hotel (also with pool), 2070 Solano Avenue (moderate).

Great America

SANTA CLARA

❦ A 360-degree swinging ship, a hair-raising, 130-foot free-fall, a 50-mile-an-hour roller coaster . . . without a doubt, Great America is the thrill-ride capital of Northern California.

Considering all the attention given the park's newest, gut-wrenching rides, like "Revolution," "Grizzly" and "The Edge," we wondered whether young children (and we adults with sensitive stomachs) would even be welcome.

Fortunately, we found this hundred-acre theme park to be as sensitive to the needs and interests of the faint at heart as it is to the fearless. Great America is a satisfying blend of fast and furious with slow and easy.

For thrill seekers, the park keeps getting better. In addition to a tried-and-true collection of rides that have been in place since Great America opened in 1976, new attractions keep bringing the bold back for more. "Revolution" is among the newest. Disguised as a docile passenger ship, the ride begins to swing like a pendulum until passengers are literally suspended upside down.

"The Edge" is a cage in which riders fall from a tall tower, straight down along a track at about 55 miles per hour. There's also "Demon," a sleek, high-speed "special effects" roller coaster, and "Grizzly," a classic, wooden roller coaster based on a Coney Island ride of yesteryear.

While the adventurous are off careening, soaring and spinning, the less courageous members of your family won't be left out. Two areas of the park are particular havens for the young set. At "Fort Fun," kids can meet various well-known costumed cartoon characters or gather round an imaginative marionette theater called the "Puppet Tree." Rides with mild-mannered names like "Little Dodge 'Em," "Yakki Doodle's Lady Bugs" and "Huck's Hang Gliders" provide a training ground for the more awesome attractions to which little kids will ultimately graduate.

Nearby "Smurf Woods," named after the little blue cartoon stars, is home to the "Blue Streak," a mini–roller coaster that tops out at 25 miles per hour. Other small-fry rides are also located here.

Live entertainment is always a major focus at Great America, and there's usually some type of professional show under way. Guests might catch an indoor musical, a rock band at the outdoor amphi-

An ornate double-deck carousel is Great America's centerpiece.

theater, performing dolphins at the aquatic show or a giant-screen movie in the "Pictorium."

In all their attempts to entertain, the management hasn't lost sight of the basics. For parents with young children, Great America comes through with some needed niceties. An infant-care area for changing diapers is provided, as are stroller rental and a lost-children's center to reunite separated kids and parents.

Great America, Great America Parkway at Highway 101 (mailing address: P.O. Box 1776), Santa Clara, CA 95052. Telephone (408) 988-1800. Five miles north of San Jose on Highway 101; 45 miles south of San Francisco. One admission price includes unlimited use of rides as well as shows and attractions. Special rates offered for young children. Parking fee. Stroller rentals available. Open daily during summer months; weekends during spring and fall. Call for specific hours.

Spending the Night?

The nearby Doubletree Hotel (Santa Clara) has a heated swimming pool and spa, as well as a health club. Moderate to expensive.

The Days Inn also has a pool and spa. Moderate. The Marriott Hotel offers four tennis courts, two pools (one indoor), exercise room and spa. Moderate to expensive. All three are located on Great America Parkway, a short distance from the park.

Santa Cruz
Beach Boardwalk
SANTA CRUZ

🐭 During the summer months, El Sol acts as a powerful magnet, luring tens of thousands of Santa Clara and San Joaquin Valley folks over twisting Highway 17 to California's remaining genuine seaside amusement park. The Santa Cruz Beach Boardwalk has entertained generations of fun and sun seekers since opening day back in 1907. Where else can you find a carousel and roller coaster listed as national historic landmarks?

Admission to the Boardwalk is free. Families buy either tickets for individual rides or an all-day, unlimited pass good for the park's more than two dozen rides. These range from the "Giant Dipper" (rated among the world's 10 best roller coasters) to smaller, kiddie-type rides. Of interest to both young and old is a vintage carousel

The Santa Cruz Beach Boardwalk is the lone survivor of California's once famous string of beachfront amusement parks.

with 70 hand-carved, gleaming horses that whirl to the sound of an antique Ruth band organ built before the turn of the century.

In between rides, you'll also find enough cotton candy and salt-water taffy stands to keep the sweetest tooth in your group happy. A number of shops, too, are situated along this classic promenade.

The indoor miniature-golf course used to be a salt-water pool that was a principal boardwalk attraction during the early years. Although the pool has long since been filled in, some relics still are in use. Stroll through the penny arcade and you'll see coin-operated games that your grandmother might have played in her youth.

An expansion and renovation program a few years ago brought a new pirate-ship swing ride and a rejuvenated Coconut Grove, a classic old-style ballroom that still occasionally hosts big bands. A Sunday brunch is held under a huge retractable glass ceiling.

The Boardwalk fronts a mile-long gentle swimming beach that is regularly cleaned and sifted by the park's maintenance crews.

Santa Cruz Beach Boardwalk, 400 Beach Street, Santa Cruz, CA 95060. Telephone (408) 423-5590. Take Highway 1 or 17 into Santa Cruz and follow signs to Santa Cruz Beach. Santa Cruz is 70 miles south of San Francisco. The Boardwalk is open daily during the summer and on weekends and holidays during the spring and fall.

The "Giant Dipper" at Santa Cruz is rated one of the world's top ten roller coasters.

Columbia State Historic Park

TUOLUMNE COUNTY

❦ If you're tired of coaxing school-weary children to "another boring museum" for a peek into California's colorful past, it's time to consider a different approach. Columbia State Historic Park outside Sonora in Tuolumne County is a history lesson in disguise. On our last visit, the kids learned about blacksmithing, gold mining, early transportation and Gold Rush life—without even realizing it.

Unlike many of the Mother Lode's Gold Rush hamlets where the old often clashes with the new, time—for all appearances' sake—stopped long ago in Columbia. The state stepped in around 1945 and designated the once-thriving old mining town a state historic park, thus preserving a bit of one of the state's most important eras.

Although much of the town has been reconstructed, it was done faithfully. The absence of motorized vehicles on the town's main streets lends a further air of authenticity to the scene. Much more than a series of false-fronted old buildings, Columbia is a thriving community, offering a number of tourist-oriented attractions and things to do for families.

For most, a visit is incomplete without a ride on the stagecoach around the town and countryside. There are lots of wide little eyes when, midway through the trip, a costumed robber stages a mock hold-up. (Our kids were ready to hand over their Mickey Mouse watches.)

In keeping with the Gold Rush atmosphere, a "smithy" practices his craft in a cluttered blacksmith shop downtown, personalizing horseshoes for a fee. Elsewhere, a re-creation of a Gold Rush–era home hints at the austere lifestyle of the forty-niners.

At the city saloon, kids can order a sarsaparilla and adults can relax with a cold beer. Other displays here include a museum, Chinese store, an old fire truck and the "fandango hall" where the earlier citizens kicked up their heels after a hard day working the mines. Even the old Columbia jail is open for inspection. The hands-down favorite attraction, however, is the Columbia Candy Kitchen, where hand-dipped chocolates and scores of other tempting goodies have been made for four generations.

After a day of prowling the bustling downtown area, you may want to get away from the crowds and take the short walk (or drive) up the hill to the century-old, two-story Columbia School, restored several years ago to its original state, right down to the hickory switches and dunce cap. If you're lucky enough to visit when a volunteer school marm is present, you and your family can stroll through the classroom and examine the old educational paraphernalia. After a taste of readin', writin' and 'rithmetic in the Gold Rush era, chances are kids will have a better appreciation for their contemporary classrooms come Monday morning.

Columbia State Historic Park is just north of Sonora off Highway 49, about 75 miles east of Stockton. For further information, contact the Tuolumne County Visitors Bureau at (209) 984-INFO.

Spending the Night?

The City Hotel and Fallon Hotel are 1850's-era hostelries that have been restored and decorated with period furnishings. Rooms have half-baths, with showers down the hall. Moderate.

Down the road a bit is the Columbia Gem Motel, a collection of cottages among pine trees. Less expensive to moderate.

The Columbia Inn Motel has a swimming pool and multi-bedroom units. Less expensive to moderate.

Southern California

❦

Hearst Castle

SAN SIMEON

❦ One of the joys of children getting older (in addition to saying goodbye to diapers) is being able to expand family travel horizons. While some adventurous parents don't hesitate to pack small children off to places where mountain goats fear to tread, we generally postponed such trips until our kids could truly enjoy them.

Hearst Castle is one of these destinations.

The palatial estate of publishing magnate William Randolph Hearst, this hilltop compound was constructed over a period of about 30 years. The result is one of California's most awe-inspiring man-made wonders, with more than three dozen bedrooms, almost as many baths, two libraries and a movie theater. Hearst reportedly spent $50 million on art alone.

Given to the state in 1959 and now operated by the Department of Parks and Recreation, the Hearst San Simeon State Historical Monument has hosted more than 20 million visitors.

Ticket holders are taken from a new Visitor Center along Highway 1 to the top of the hill in busses, and led through the gardens and buildings in groups by well-informed guides.

Four different tours are offered. Probably the most popular is Tour One, which includes stops at an opulent guest house, several garden

William Randolph Hearst's palatial estate is a favorite among families with strong legs.

areas, the magnificent outdoor Neptune pool and indoor Roman pool and the ground floor of the castle proper, including assembly room, refectory, morning room, billiard room and theater (climbing 150 steps in all).

Those on Tour Two stroll through an Italian-style suite, three guest rooms, library, Hearst's own suite, "Celestial Suite," "Della Robbia Room," pantry and hotellike kitchen (climbing 356 steps in all).

Tour Three covers a small guest house, the pools, the castle's newest wing, built during the owner's final years, and the mix of architectural styles represented in the estate (climbing 300 steps).

On Tour Four, visitors are treated to a more extensive look at the formal gardens as well as a hidden terrace, wine cellar, a guest house and pools (climbing 283 steps).

For those who haven't been to the castle before, Tour One is a good choice. Compared to the other routes, it has half as many steps. And, because more than twice as many people squeeze in to Tour One, an occasional whine is much less conspicuous. However, the guide's discussion, both in the bus (recorded) and during the walk, is oriented to adults and older children who have an interest in subjects ranging from regional flora to Italian art. Further, the six-minute movie shown in the castle theater is a sleeper for young kids. The film shows movie stars long since departed frolicking at the castle during its early years. It's a welcome opportunity to rest tired little legs, though.

While young ones may be bored by most of the verbiage, they seem to take great delight in the new visual feast around every corner. The tour moves quickly, and the scenery changes as rapidly. One minute you're staring down on the enchanted Neptune pool and the next you're peering along a dining table that looks like something right out of King Arthur's castle.

Although the state posts no limitations with respect to age (strollers, however, are not permitted), we saw few preschool-aged children on our trip. Those who appeared to be in the age-six-or older range generally had little or no trouble navigating the many steps or keeping up with the group. An outdoor rest along the walking route does offer a chance for a drink of water and a brief opportunity to sit a spell. (All the tours are about a half-mile in length, and each takes just under two hours.)

Restroom facilities, food and souvenirs are available at the Visitors Center. Restoration of some of the castle art can also be viewed here.

Before you make the drive to San Simeon, make sure you've got tour reservations. Californians can make reservations by calling toll-free (800) 446-PARK.

Hearst San Simeon State Historical Monument, San Simeon, CA. For reservations, call the above number in California or (619) 452-1950, or write to MISTIX, P.O. Box 85705, San Diego, CA 92138-5705. Children under six are free if seated on a parental lap in the bus. Hearst Castle is located on Highway 1, about 42 miles north of San

Luis Obispo. Driving time from either Los Angeles or San Francisco is about six hours.

Spending the Night?

See San Simeon Pines Resort listing in Part I.

Diversions

Hearst State Beach is just across the highway. Motorists who scoot through Cambria on Highway 101 without detouring through the quaint village are missing lots of interesting arts and crafts shops and an atmosphere reminiscent of the 1960's.

Santa Monica Pier
SANTA MONICA

🍒 Despite occasional battles with brash Pacific storms, the venerable Santa Monica Pier has stood the test of time. Built in 1908, the pier was the site of the famous La Monica Ballroom, where thousands danced summer nights away to big band sounds. During those early years the pier also boasted a giant roller coaster and an ornate, hand-carved carousel.

The newly restored carousel with 46 colorful horses is one of the remaining attractions of the old days. Still, the pier remains one of the south coast's most enduring attractions. Today's pier amusements are more reminiscent of the county-fair circuit, consisting of bumper cars, arcades, the carousel and food stands.

Although the winter storms of 1983 ravaged portions of the pier, Santa Monicans weren't about to let their pride and joy slip beneath the sea. The city formed a nonprofit corporation that has restored much of the structure.

Thanks to strong civic pride, the pier's future looks bright. Now, if we could only do something about those storms.

Santa Monica Pier, end of Colorado Boulevard on Ocean Avenue.

From the Santa Monica Freeway, take the 4th/5th Street (north) exit and turn left on Colorado Boulevard. Fishing, amusements, antique carousel, food stands and occasional entertainment.

Six Flags
Magic Mountain

VALENCIA

❦ At the risk of being labeled a wimp (or worse), I'll admit to not being a fan of thrill rides. While my boyhood friends rode roller coasters free-handed and rocked their Ferris wheel seats into nearly 360-degree turns, I looked on squeamishly from below, planted squarely on terra firma. I developed vicarious stomach aches just watching. My sentiments haven't changed; if I wanted to test my G-force resistance, I'd be piloting a space shuttle instead of a typewriter. Consequently, my observations of Six Flags Magic Mountain's more wild rides are those of an observer rather than a participant. But it doesn't take a connoisseur of rides to understand why Magic Mountain is a thrill-rider's paradise.

Consider just a few of the more wild and crazy, er, amusements. The "Z-Force" looping fighter jet stalls upside down about a hundred feet off the ground just before pulling 3 G's as it dives into 360-degree loops. "Shock Wave" is a stand-up, looping roller coaster that tops out at the highway speed of my car. Riders on "Freefall" sit in padded gondolas as they move to the top of a 10-story tower and drop at a rate of speed experienced only by skydivers.

I'll leave it to your imagination to infer why other rides bear such names as "Revolution," "Log Jammer," "Jet Stream" and "Crazy Barrels." I've had enough.

Fortunately, younger ones (and timid adults) aren't overlooked here for a minute. For the pre-thrill-ride set, there's a lot to do. "Bugs Bunny World" is a popular destination. Kids can hug a costumed cartoon character, slide into pint-sized cars or dune buggies, explore a pirate ship or ride mini–prop planes. There's also a petting zoo in the park.

After a few hours of riding and running around, families often head for one of Magic Mountain's live shows. During your visit, programs

For the pre-thrill-ride set, Magic Mountain's "Bugs Bunny World" is where the action is.

might include a rock concert, fireworks show, wild animal show, dolphin or sea lion show or a cartoon character circus.

In all, the park offers more than a hundred rides and shows, a crafts village, dance club, big-name entertainment and eateries.

Oh, on your next visit, look for me. I'm the guy either sitting on the bench with his head between his knees or trying to pass the four-foot height limit in order to steal a hug from Bugs.

Six Flags Magic Mountain, 26101 Magic Mountain Parkway, Valencia, CA 91355. Telephone (818) 992-0884 or (805) 255-4100. From Interstate 5, take Magic Mountain Parkway. Children under 48 inches get a break on general admission. Parking is extra. The park is generally open daily from late May through mid-September, and weekends and school holidays the rest of the year. Call for specific hours.

Spending the Night?

The Best Western Ranch House Inn offers swimming and wading pools and a free shuttle to Magic Mountain (across the street).

Santa's Village

SKYFOREST

❦ Ever wonder where Santa spends the off-season? While the elves are burning the midnight oil up north, Saint Nick is taking it easy at his mountain retreat in the San Bernardino National Forest.

For the past 20 or so years, little ones have been trooping up to Santa's Village to catch an early peek at the jolly one, enjoy a day of fun and maybe drop a couple of hints for next Christmas. A family-operated amusement park, Santa's Village was built to resemble the North Pole, with colorful log buildings and "snow" on the grounds. The village is designed to appeal primarily to kids between the ages of 2 and 12. General admission gives visitors free run of the village and unlimited use of the park's dozen rides, including monorail, Cinderella's pumpkin coach, a Ferris wheel, sleigh, train and burro ride.

Other enticements include toy and gift shops, puppet shows, candy shop and a Christmas ornament shop. Group hay rides through the lush forest are also offered, as are birthday party packages.

And don't forget Santa. The bearded host is always nearby with reindeer and costumed elves to welcome young visitors to his mountain village. Whoever said Christmas comes but once a year obviously didn't live in Southern California.

Santa's Village, P.O. Box 638, Skyforest, CA 92385. Telephone (714) 337-2481. From San Bernardino, take Highway 215 north to the Mountain Resorts exit. At Waterman Avenue (Highway 18), turn left and continue on to Santa's Village, about two miles past the Lake Arrowhead turnoff. Open daily from mid-June through mid-September and from mid-November until early January. Open weekends and holidays the rest of the year, except closed March through Memorial Day.

Disneyland

ANAHEIM

❦ What can we say about California's most popular family attraction that hasn't already been said—again and again? Although many of us could walk blindfolded from Tomorrowland to Adventureland, no family guidebook would be complete without including Disneyland. After all, there must be at least a couple of California families who haven't found their way here—yet.

Growing up may have meant giving up many juvenile pursuits, but Disneyland fortunately isn't among them. Children of the 1950's who enjoyed the park in their youth and who are now returning with their own kids are proof positive that you never outgrow this place. Indeed, on our family's last visit, I'm not sure who had the most fun: the children or we old veterans.

While the younger generation would like to think they hold exclusive reign over the Magic Kingdom, those of us who cut our teeth on the Matterhorn bobsleds and Tom Sawyer's treehouse know a thing or two. We were Disneyland's first generation.

We know the short cuts, the best restaurants, the most interesting shops and which attractions are most likely to have the longest lines. The park's "magic" won't get you to the front of a line any quicker, but that doesn't stop visitors from developing their own strategies for dealing with long waits. Some are more successful than others.

We've found that folks often try to avoid the inevitable queues by

The riverboat Mark Twain *rounds the bend near New Orleans Square.*

arriving early and heading straight away for the most popular attractions. We avoided that frenzy, instead devoting the morning and much of the afternoon to other rides where the wait was minimal. As the hour gets later, the crowds usually begin to thin. We took in "Star Tours" just before closing time when the line was half as long as it was during much of the day.

Others try to avoid the crowds altogether by visiting during the off-season. It's a Catch-22 situation. Although the park is quieter during the school year, many of Disneyland's special events and celebrations, as well as extended evening hours, are reserved for the summer months.

In the final analysis, Disneyland is a great place to visit any time of year. The images of our smiling, wide-eyed children embracing

Mickey Mouse and spinning around on the tea-party cups linger in our memories long after our blistered feet have recovered.

Disneyland, 1313 South Harbor Boulevard, Anaheim, CA 92803. Telephone (714) 999-4565. From Interstate 5 or 15, take the Harbor Boulevard exit (south). Hours of operation change through the year. Call for specifics. Multiday discounted "passports" as well as guided tours are available. A single admission price includes unlimited use of attractions except arcades. Parking is extra.

Knott's Berry Farm

BUENA PARK

🐾 Long before computerized video games and knock-your-socks-off special effects brought amusement parks into a new era, Walter and Cordelia Knott were packing them in with good, old-fashioned fun and food. Among the nation's theme parks, this is the granddaddy of them all.

The "farm" traces its history from humble beginnings. First there was Walter's 1920's roadside berry stand. (He was the first to market the boysenberry.) Then Cordelia opened a restaurant and began serving up tasty chicken dinners. Later, as entertainment for the waiting restaurant patrons, a replica of an Old West town was added. Gradually, Knott's Berry Farm evolved into America's first family theme park.

The authentic old buildings, many of them moved piece by piece from desert ghost towns during the 1940's, are still here, forming one of four theme areas within the park.

Among the younger set, the most popular area is Camp Snoopy, home of the characters from the comic strip "Peanuts." Attractions here include suspension bridges, kiddie rides and live shows. Visitors often get a chance to meet a costumed Charlie Brown, Snoopy or other neighborhood "Peanuts" friends.

The Roaring 20's area is the setting for "Kingdom of the Dinosaurs," one of the park's newest rides. Guests ride through a prehistoric jungle inhabited by a number of lifelike dinosaurs and other creatures.

The popular dinosaur attraction was among several added during a recent multimillion-dollar expansion program that brought the park new thrill rides and a 3-D movie. Rides here range from a 20-story parachute sky jump to a fast-moving thriller called "Montezooma's Revenge."

Throughout the day there's live entertainment in the form of the "Calico Cancan Show," Wild West stunt show and aquatic programs at Pacific Pavilion.

With the wild rides and high-tech trappings of newer California amusement parks, Knott's Berry Farm is giving today's younger generation just what it has come to expect. However, the bazaars of Fiesta Village and gold panning at the park's ghost town contribute to a nostalgic feeling that will remind parents of simpler times. Walter Knott's park is an example of progress with respect for the past.

Knott's Berry Farm, 8039 Beach Boulevard, Buena Park, CA 90620. Telephone (714) 220-5200. From Interstate 5, exit on La Palma and drive west to the park. From Highway 91, take Beach Boulevard. (Highway 39) south. The park is 10 minutes from Disneyland. Knott's Berry Farm is open every day except Christmas. Call for specific hours. Single admission includes unlimited use of attractions.

Tournament of Roses Parade

PASADENA

🐭 For many Californians (and Americans, for that matter), New Year's Day without the Tournament of Roses Parade is like a birthday cake without candles.

Most of us—about 125 million at last count—view this annual event on TV from the comfort of our family rooms. However, another million folks opt to watch the parade unfold in person. For kids whose in-person exposure to parades is limited to small-town Fourth of July pageants, a trip to Pasadena will be an eye-opening adventure he or she isn't likely to forget.

In all, some 60 floats, 20 or so bands and more than 225 equestrians take part in the parade. The average float consists of a hundred thousand flowers and upwards of a million petals. The result is a colorful and aromatic display unlike anything most young people have ever seen.

Weather isn't usually a problem. Organizers say Mother Nature has rained on this parade only a half-dozen or so times since the event began in 1890.

The challenge is finding a spot from which to get a good view. Staking a curbside claim more than one day before the parade is unlawful, but that doesn't seem to stop the squatters who begin scouting choice spots along the route just after Christmas. Obviously, most families will find camping out on the streets of Pasadena impractical. The best bet is to shell out a few dollars for seats in the grandstand. Be sure to order by spring for best seating next year.

Following are a few tips for a successful trip. The parade is held January 1 unless New Year's falls on Sunday. In that case, the parade and Rose Bowl Game are held on Monday, January 2.

The parade begins at 8:30 A.M. and lasts about two hours. The route starts on South Orange Grove Boulevard and continues east along famous Colorado Boulevard to Sierra Madre Boulevard, where the floats are displayed until the following day. Grandstands are erected along Colorado Boulevard. Ticket information is available by calling the Pasadena Convention and Visitors Bureau at (818) 795-9311.

If you're driving to the parade, know where your seats are and park as close as possible. Plan to park by 6:30 A.M. Should you find yourself in a predawn traffic snarl, don't mutter that you "should have watched the parade at home." You won't be able to smell the roses on TV.

Spending the Night?

Be advised that although there are numerous hotels and motels within a short distance of the parade route, many require a three-to-five-night stay, payable in advance. The Convention and Visitors Bureau (phone number above) will send you a list of local lodgings.

Diversions

Those who arrive a few days in advance of the parade have the opportunity to watch the floats being constructed at several sites. The best time is two days prior to the event. The Tournament of

Roses Association publishes a brochure listing locations, hours and admission charges.

Kidspace is a "participatory" museum where young folks are encouraged to touch and learn. Included in this Pasadena museum are a TV studio, live ant colony and the "KFUN DeeJay Booth." (It's further described under Memorable Museums, in Part III.) Brookside Park on Rosemont Avenue has two 18-hole golf courses, swimming, tennis and other recreational facilities. The Pasadena Ice Skating Center is on East Green Street.

Universal Studios Tour
UNIVERSAL CITY

🐭 For parents and kids with even a passing interest in movies or TV, a ride through Universal Studios' famous back lot is like finding buried treasure. Hop aboard a tour tram and within a couple of hours you'll visit Beaver Cleaver's street, the Bates Motel (from *Psycho*), King Kong's New York City, the New England town terrorized by *Jaws* and even the Red Sea, with a side trip through the Old West.

On this bus, getting there is 90 percent of the fun. Barely around the first turn, your tram is "blasted" by weird creatures piloting an alien tank, and visitors find themselves in the midst of a laser war.

Driving back in time, the tram approaches "Brooklyn" when King Kong appears and begins to wreak havoc with the bridge you're crossing. Recovering from a wild slide, the bus beats a hasty retreat from TV's "Bionic Woman" toward the collapsing bridge. Through some impressive hydraulic gyrations the bridge seems to give way beneath you, only to quickly rebuild itself for the next bus.

The remainder of the trip promises a run-in with the famous movie shark Jaws, a ride through the parted waters of the Red Sea inspired by the film *The Ten Commandments* and an equilibrium-jarring journey through an ice cave.

Along the way, visitors make a series of stops for a backstage look at how TV shows and movies are made. There's a visit to a special-effects stage, a flashy eye-opening program called "The Adventures of Conan," a western stunt show, the animal-actors stage and, probably the tour's most popular attraction, "Screen Test Comedy Theatre." Several tour guests are selected to star in a short videotaped production that utilizes just about every famous film cliche in the book, along with bits and pieces of real movies thrown in for an extra laugh. The finished product is played back to the audience, including the red-faced "actors."

At the Entertainment Center, a number of displays will catch the eye of any child familiar with television. "K.I.T.T.," the talking car from "Knight Rider," will speak to your kids, while costumed characters from Charlie Chaplin and Frankenstein to Woody Woodpecker are happy to pose for pictures.

If you're interested in gazing at movie stars and seeing real movies being filmed, you'll have better luck elsewhere. The Universal Studios Tour is more an entertaining, action-packed tribute to Hollywood than a nuts-and-bolts lesson in filmmaking. Still, the tour ranks among the top tourist attractions in the U.S., and four million people a year can't be all wrong.

Universal Studios Tour, 100 Universal City Plaza, Universal City, CA 91608. Telephone (818) 508-9600. From the Hollywood Freeway (Highway 101), take either the Barham Boulevard or Lankershim Boulevard exit. Tours run daily except on Thanksgiving and Christmas. Call for specific hours. Tours consist of a two-and-a-half-hour guided tram excursion through movie lots and several live-action shows. Children under three are free.

San Diego Wild Animal Park

ESCONDIDO

🐾 We know folks who have spent small fortunes for an African photo safari. But hey, why shell out thousands of dollars when (for two adults and two young children) you can have a similar experience in Southern California for less than 50 bucks?

The San Diego Wild Animal Park, country outpost of the nonprofit San Diego Zoo, is an 1800-acre wildlife preserve where scores of animals, many in herds, roam among sprawling biogeographical enclosures that replicate their exotic homelands of Africa and Asia.

Unlike zoos where visitors view animals from black-topped walkways through cages, the animal park offers a chance to see creatures in a more natural setting. You might see a baby critter being born or two sheep locking horns.

Visitors board the silent, nonpolluting "Wgasa Bush Line" monorail for a five-mile, 50-minute narrated tour along a track that winds past mountain gorillas, Asian lions, Sumatran tigers, elephants, giraffes, rhinoceroses and water buffalo.

For the more adventurous, the park offers specially arranged "photo caravans" that transport visitors in open-air trucks into the field preserve for close-up pictures that will rival those taken by your friends in Africa.

For the energetic, there's also the "Kilimanjaro Trail," a one-plus-mile walking trail that affords more leisurely viewing of some of the park's larger residents, among them cheetahs, antelope, tigers and lions. The "Australian Rain Forest," also situated along the path, is home to hundreds of South Pacific plant, bird and animal species.

The park wouldn't be complete without animal shows. Visitors can watch performing parrots, intelligent elephants and rare critters. (More than 20 endangered species have reproduced at the park.) Elephant rides are also offered, and a kiddie "kraal" allows little people a chance to pet little animals.

What do you do when you're on safari, it's hot and the kids are hungry? Just stroll on over to the nearby jungle hut in the park's "Nairobi Village" and order a "super safari cone." While such indulgences aren't available in the real African bush, the San Diego Wild Animal Park goes out of its way to provide the creature comforts — along with the creatures.

San Diego Wild Animal Park, 15500 San Pasqual Valley Road, Escondido, CA 92027-9614. Telephone (619) 480-0100 or (619) 747-8702. From Interstate 15 south of Escondido, take Via Rancho Parkway and follow signs to park. Guided monorail tours; walking, self-guided tour; animal shows and rides. Special photo caravan and behind-the-scenes tours available by reservation. Fast-food outlets and gift shops. Rental strollers available. Open all year. Call for specific hours. Single admission includes monorail ride and shows.

San Diego Zoo

SAN DIEGO

❦ When the Panama-California Exposition folded its tents back in 1916, it left behind—in San Diego's Balboa Park—a bear, some wolves and a few lions. From that modest menagerie has grown one of America's foremost family attractions. In fact, for many folks it's hard to say *San Diego* without saying *zoo*.

As a small-town kid growing up in central California, my idea of a zoo was a row of cramped, smelly cages holding a couple of pacing foxes and a few aging monkeys. The San Diego Zoo, on the other hand, is home to more than three thousand animals, many representing the largest collections ever assembled.

Because of the vastness of the zoo, you might consider taking the 40-minute guided bus tour, which winds up mesas and down valleys, covering three miles. The open-sided busses leave the zoo station every few minutes. After the tour, you can always retrace your path to places of particular interest.

The "Skyfari" aerial tram offers a different perspective, taking visitors above the treetops for a bird's-eye view of "Monkey Mesa," ape grottos and sea lion pool.

Another way to see the zoo is through a behind-the-scenes tour. The "Inside Story" includes a slide show and takes visitors into food warehouses and an animal "bedroom," and offers a chance to touch some unusual zoo critters. Two- and three-hour versions of the tour are scheduled daily, and reservations are required.

The children's zoo is built to the scale of four-year-olds, enabling little people and animals to see eye to eye. In addition to direct-contact areas, the children's zoo is the site of a popular glass-fronted nursery where young primates and small animals are bottle-fed and diapered. Elsewhere in the zoo are elephant and camel rides, as well as various animal shows.

Our youngsters grew jealous hearing about the zoo's educational programs, which each year bring thousands of San Diego school children to the facility for guided tours. After all, in our town, a field trip to the corner bakery is a major excursion.

San Diego Zoo, Balboa Park (mailing address: P.O. Box 551), San Diego, CA 92112-0551. Telephone (619) 234-3153. Both Interstate 5 and Highway 163 run through the park. The zoo is on Zoo Drive. Three thousand animals representing eight hundred species.

Guided bus tour and aerial tram ride available (extra charge for aerial tram). Animal rides, children's zoo, animal shows, fast-food outlets and gift shop. Stroller rentals available. The zoo is open daily. Call for specific hours.

Sea World

SAN DIEGO

✓ When it comes to getting close to marine life, Californians have myriad opportunities. Still, there's no place quite like San Diego's Sea World. Others must agree, since this "ocean-arium" has consistently placed second only to Disneyland among the state's most popular family attractions.

Even if you've visited California's other marine-life attractions, Sea World won't be a letdown. Indeed, if you've already toured the park, you'll likely find something new on a return trip. Recent additions include "Shamu Stadium," site of the famous killer-whale show, and the largest marine mammal facility ever built. "Places of Learning" is a recently constructed educational complex consisting of a one-acre walking map of the U.S., a giant chess board, large-scale replicas of classic children's books and a store specializing in educational toys.

The longer-running attractions continue to pack 'em in as well. There's always a crowd at "Penguin Encounter," where more than four hundred birds live in separate environments ranging from a simulated Antarctic ice shelf to a re-creation of a volcanic island.

While lots of kids have hugged farm animals at petting zoos, touching and feeding dolphins at Sea World's unique petting pool will likely be a new experience for most. Another treat for the young set is "Cap'n Kids' World," an area containing small-scale rides and play equipment.

In addition to the tried and true performances by the park's otters, sea lions and other creatures of the deep, there are now shows featuring people. "City Streets" is a musical variety show set in a re-creation of a city neighborhood, and "Muscle Beach" stars an all-human high-dive act.

Elsewhere in the park, a sky ride takes visitors to the top of a 320-

We're all familiar with petting zoos. At Sea World there's a petting pool.

foot tower for a revolving view of San Diego. You can also enjoy Mission Bay from either a gondola cable car or a zooming hydrofoil.

When all is said and done, it's the marine life that will make the most enduring impression. In glittery Southern California, where famous entertainers usually sport human form, Sea World has made full-fledged stars out of fish. Just don't ask a killer whale for an autograph. That's one task Shamu hasn't mastered—yet.

Sea World, 1720 South Shores Road, San Diego, CA 92109-9980. Telephone (619) 226-3901. From Interstate 5, exit at Sea World Drive (west). Open daily. Call park for hours. Seven shows, 30 educational exhibits, three rides and four aquariums. Fast-food outlets throughout the park. Single admission includes all shows and exhibits. Free parking. Strollers available.

III

Daytripping
and Other
Diversions

🍎 The weekend's coming, your brood is bored and you're searching for a good place to head for a day trip – somewhere new and exciting; a spot not too far from home that you've always meant to visit or maybe a destination you've completely overlooked.

A Civil War–era fort, perhaps? A train ride through the coastal forests? How about a walk (or crawl) through a foothill cavern or a tour of a real chocolate factory?

The adventures listed in the following pages are perfect for day trips, or for overnighters in conjunction with a visit to one of the destinations in the first part of this book

Except for the ski resorts, which are grouped clearly in Northern or Southern California, and the festivities, which are organized by season of the year, the day-trip destinations in each section are listed roughly from north to south.

Skiing and
Snow Play

❦ Anyone who thinks California is strictly sun, sand and surf hasn't spent a whole year here. Contrary to the stereotypical image of the Golden State, we do get our share of the white stuff—which makes for some great recreation, whether your idea of winter family fun means building a snowman or roaring down a 3,600-foot vertical drop on a pair of skis.

Before you go charging blindly up to the mountains, here's a sampling of resorts that take good care of kids, as well as tips for finding a good place to pitch a few snowballs.

Snow Play Areas

The California Department of Parks and Recreation operates more than a dozen winter snow play areas up and down the state. (Snowmobiles are welcome at select sites.) Use is by permit only, and season passes are available. You may request a listing of current locales by writing to "Sno-Park," P.O. Box 942896, Sacramento 94296-0001, or by calling (916) 322-8993 (for a recorded message) or (916) 322-8593 (to reach a real voice).

Wee skiers stick together at Alpine Meadows.

Ski Resorts

NORTHERN CALIFORNIA

Lassen Volcanic National Park Ski Area
(916) 595-3376

The children's ski package includes lesson, rentals, lift ticket and lunch.

Squaw Valley
Tahoe west shore
(916) 583-6955 or 583-4743

Specialized programs include the "Ten Little Indians" ski school, "Junior Ski School" and a child-care program for infants and toddlers.

Heavenly Valley
South Lake Tahoe
(916) 541-SKII or
(707) 588-4584

"SKI Wee" program is designed for kids age (approximately) 12 and younger. Lunch is included in package.

Homewood
Tahoe west shore
(916) 525-7256

Children age four to six may take a one-hour "Kiddie School" lesson. Young hotdoggers may join a junior racing team. Other learn-to-ski packages are also offered.

Alpine Meadows
Tahoe City
(916) 583-4232

Alpine's "Children's Snow School" has a fine reputation for teaching three-to-six-year-olds how to ski. Packages include rentals, indoor and outdoor supervision, snacks and lunch.

Northstar-at-Tahoe
Truckee
(916) 562-1010

Northstar offers child care as well as instruction. See separate listing in Part I of this book for details.

Boreal Ridge
Truckee
(916) 426-3666

A day-care program and "Children's Ski School" are offered at this family-oriented resort. The "Animal Crackers" day-care center features snow play, snacks and supervision.

Sierra Ski Ranch
Twin Bridges (south Tahoe area)
(916) 659-7519

Included in the resort's ski curriculum is the "Sierra Super Skiers" program for kids age 4 to 12. Indoor child-care is also offered.

Kirkwood
Thirty miles south of Lake Tahoe
(209) 258-6000

Kirkwood's programs for kids include the "Rainbow Children's Center" (ages 3 to 8) and "Mighty Mountain" children's ski school (ages 4 to 12).

Mount Reba/Bear Valley
Central Sierra area
(209) 753-2301

This resort offers a learn-to-ski money-back guarantee, as well as a "Skiing Bears" instructional program for children.

Badger Pass
Yosemite National Park
(209) 372-1300

The ski school at this family resort is the oldest in the west. If you don't learn to ski in one day, they'll give you another day's package free. There's also a "Ski Tots Room" for kids.

Sierra Summit
Lakeshore (central Sierra area)
(209) 893-3316

Day care as well as instruction are offered at this resort, located about 65 miles north of Fresno.

SOUTHERN CALIFORNIA

Mammoth Mountain
Mammoth Lakes
(619) 934-2571

June Mountain
Mammoth Lakes
(619) 648-7733

These co-owned resorts offer day care as well as a range of instructional programs geared for kids, including "Fun Land" ski school and the "Woolly Mammoth" school.

Snow Summit
Big Bear Lake
(714) 866-5766

The "Kiddy School" (ages 4 to 8) and "Children's Ski School" (ages 9 to 12) are the special programs here for youngsters.

Goldmine
Big Bear Lake
(714) 585-2519

This is a family favorite, known for its "Miner's Camp" and "SKI Wee" program.

Snow Valley
Running Springs
(714) 867-2751

Southern California's largest ski area doesn't ignore the younger set. There are special rates and special programs for children.

Mount Baldy
West of San Bernardino
(714) 982-0800

There's a "Kiddie Ski School" and a beginner's special that includes all the necessities, including a half-day lesson.

Ski Sunrise
Wrightwood
(619) 249-6150

The "Small Fry" program is operated for children age three to seven, and children under five ski free.

Mountain High
Wrightwood
(619) 249-5471

An easily accessible south-state resort, Mountain High welcomes kids with its "Children's Buckeroo Program."

Water Parks

❦ If you don't mind bathing with literally hundreds (sometimes thousands) of strangers, you'll find water parks, which are relatively new California hot-weather diversions, quite exciting. (As a kid, all I had was a tree swing over the creek.) Most combine thrilling chutes and flumes, which are more popular with older kids and adults, with calm tubing and wading areas that appeal to younger swimmers.

Following are 12 of the state's best. Call for admission and hours.

Waterworks Park
Redding
(916) 246-9550

Just off Interstate 5 in one of California's warmest locales.

Windsor Waterworks and Slides
Conde Lane, Windsor
(707) 838-7760

Waterplay in the wine country, just north of Santa Rosa.

Waterworld USA
Cal Expo at Interstate
(Business) 80, Sacramento
(916) 924-0555

This newly revamped park shares the grounds of Cal Expo, site of the state fair.

Oakwood Lake Water ThemePark
On Highway 120 between Highway 99 and Interstate 5, Manteca
(209) 239-9566

Manteca's claim to fame offers several slides and rapids. Located north of Modesto.

The Orchard Waterslide
East of State Routes 33 and 132, Modesto
(209) 523-2642

In addition to flumes and pools, this park has a campground.

Rapids Waterslide
Off Interstate 580 via Santa Rita Road, Pleasanton
(415) 829-6230

This park is in the Shadow Cliff's Recreation Area.

Splash Down Waterslide
1200 South Dempsey Road, Milpitas (408) 943-9252

Flumes, picnic facilities and video games.

Raging Waters
2333 South White Road, San Jose (408) 270-8000

There's a wonderful play pool here for kids, complete with small boats as well as the requisite daring rides.

Although water theme parks like Wild Rivers weren't around when most of us were young, we can still enjoy them with our own kids.

Clovis Lakes Water Park
11413 E. Shaw
Clovis
(209) 299-4242

Located northeast of Fresno, this park offers water slides, wave pool, children's activity center and also dry-land activities, such as horseshoes and volleyball.

Newport Dunes Aquatic Park
Pacific Coast Highway at Jamboree Road, Newport Beach
(714) 644-0510

A 20-acre lagoon where kids can navigate small boats or play with whales (not the real kind).

Wild Rivers
8800 Irvine Center Drive, Irvine
(actually Laguna Hills)
(714) 768-WILD

Twenty acres and more than 40 rides and attractions—including wave machines—in a tropical setting. This park used to be the site of Lion Country Safari.

Raging Waters
111 Via Verde, San Dimas
(714) 592-6453

A quarter-mile innertube ride with rapids is among the top attractions at this huge 40-acre park near Pomona.

Caves and Caverns

❦ While many of us are well versed with the above-ground wonders of California, how many of us have taken the time to descend into a real gold mine or the subterranean world of icicle-like stalactites and stalagmites? Don't think you'll be expected to shimmy on your belly through a claustrophobe's nightmare. These California underground wonders all have walkways and stairs that can easily be navigated by able-bodied kids and adults. However, some do offer wild, down-and-dirty spelunking if you're up (or, er, down) for it. All are open year-round. Call for specific times.

Lake Shasta Caverns
O'Brien Recreation Area,
Lake Shasta
(916) 238-2341

After a short boat ride on Lake Shasta and a bus ride up a mountain, visitors explore caverns that, prior to the carving of a bigger tunnel in the 1960's, had only been seen by die-hard spelunkers.

California Caverns
at Cave City
Mountain Ranch, Calaveras County
(209) 736-2708

Visitors to this underground wonderland see 13,000-year-old human remains, underground lakes and crystal "vines" while following the footsteps of famous naturalist John Muir and author Mark Twain. The "Trail of Lights" tour lasts 80 minutes. Intensive caving tours are also offered. Call for a map.

Gold Bug Mine
Bedford Park, Placerville
(916) 622-0832

Here's a rare chance to explore a real gold mine that saw action as recently as the 1940's. Owned by the city of Placerville, the Gold Bug is open to the public.

Moaning Cavern
Parrots Ferry Road
Vallecito, Calaveras County
(209) 736-2708

Just south of California Caverns, Moaning Cavern was first seriously explored by gold miners, although prehistoric peoples were well acquainted with the moaning sound that emanates from the entrance. You'll descend a spiral staircase into an underground "room" big enough to hold the Statue of Liberty. The traditional tour lasts 45 minutes. The "Adventure Tour" is longer and scarier. Call for a map.

Pinnacles National Monument

31 miles south of Salinas, southeast of Soledad

Ancient volcanoes formed some intriguing caves here. Picnic areas and barbeques are available.

Forestiere Underground Gardens

Highway 99 at Shaw, Fresno
(209) 275-3792

For 40 years Baldasare Forestiere excavated 10 acres of hardpan, creating a mind-boggling series of underground rooms, patios and passageways: a literal subterranean home.

Boyden Cavern

Kings Canyon Sequoia National Forest (between Barton Flat and Cedar Grove)
(209) 736-2708

An extensive, five-mile-long cavern was created here as the two-thousand-foot-high marble walls of Kings Gate slowly dissolved over a period of three hundred thousand years. Guided walking tours take 45 minutes.

La Jolla Caves

1325 Coast Boulevard, La Jolla
(619) 454-6080

These caves, unknown to many who visit this popular tourist village north of San Diego, were formed by Pacific wave action. The caves are accessible through a staircase below a local shop.

Eagle Mine

End of C Street, Julian
(619) 765-9921

This Gold Rush–era mine is open for daily tours except on Easter and Christmas. Gold panning is offered at the end of the tour. Julian is situated in the hills 60 miles northeast of San Diego.

Mitchell Caverns

Providence Mountains State Recreation Area
(619) 256-3591

If you ever find yourself a hundred miles east of Barstow, check out these one-time American Indian homes– actually limestone caverns. A walking tour runs an hour or so.

Magical Mysteries

🐭 California has its share of quirks of nature and peculiar attractions. Regardless of where you live in the state, you'll not have to drive far before running across some oddity. We've got our own geyser, a 160-room mansion with stairs leading nowhere, areas where gravity plays tricks and ancient tar pits that trapped prehistoric critters. Following are a few favorite California curiosities your family will enjoy.

La Brea Tar Pits
Wilshire Boulevard and Curson Avenue, Los Angeles
(213) 936-2230

Prehistoric creatures, thinking the pools of sticky tar were water, wandered in for their last drink. Their untimely fate has given us a detailed look at about a half-million birds, reptiles and mammals. Skeletons of some, like sabre-toothed tigers and mastodons, are displayed in the on-site museum. Kids can also feel for themselves how sticky the tar is.

Mystery Spot
Branciforte Drive, Santa Cruz
(408) 423-8897

Here's another area where gravity isn't playing with a full deck. As at Confusion Hill (see page 168), you'll watch people lean backward or sideways when they stand up, and balls that appear to roll uphill.

Winchester Mystery House
525 South Winchester Boulevard, San Jose
(408) 247-2101

Sarah Winchester (of the rifle family) kept carpenters working day and night for 38 years to build her Victorian mansion. Apparently, they all let their imaginations run wild. There's a window in a floor, stairs leading into the ceiling and doors that open to solid walls. An hour-long tour visits 110 of the 160 rooms.

Paul Bunyan and Babe preside over Trees of Mystery, one of California's more curious attractions.

Bumpass Hell

Lassen Volcanic National Park
(one mile beyond Emerald
Lake)

This area resembles a massive
witch's caldron, with mud pots,
boiling pools and other types of
intriguing manifestations of the
volcanic turbulence underground. (Although Lassen is
considered dormant, scientists
don't rule out the possibility of
future eruptions.) The Bumpass
Hell trail is 1.3 miles long.

Confusion Hill

Highway 101, Piercy,
Mendocino County
(707) 925-6456

Water that runs uphill, people
standing at weird angles. . . .
Don't even try explaining this
place to the kids. Just have fun.
There's an optional mile-long
mini-train ride into the redwoods and through a tree
tunnel.

Trees of Mystery
Highway 101, Klamath
(707) 482-5613

This is an unusual nature trail
that takes walkers past a dozen
living trees supported by one
trunk (called the "Family Tree"),
a tree shaped like a lightning
bolt and the "Upside Down
Tree." The stories of Paul
Bunyan come to life through a
series of redwood sculptures
(made by nature) at the end of
the hike.

Old Faithful Geyser
(of California)
Tubbs Lane, Calistoga
(707) 942-6463

Why go to Yellowstone when
you can tour the California
wine country and stop in at the
state's own version of Old Faithful? This one is fed by an
underground river that erupts
about every 40 minutes, sending a spray of 350-degree water
high into the air.

Forts and Castles

❦ The childhood forts my friends and I built were patterned after those we'd seen in movie westerns, our castles based on passages from fairy tales. Not until later did I realize that California has a few real-life examples of each.

Fort Humboldt
Fort Avenue near Highway 101, Eureka
(707) 443-7952

Gen. U. S. Grant served a stint here during the 1850's but the fort's military history is overshadowed by an emphasis on the lumber industry, with railroad and Native American exhibits included as well.

Fort Ross
Highway 1 (north of Jenner), Sonoma County
(707) 847-3286

This former Russian outpost— now a state historic park—hints at that country's interesting architecture. Before the Gold Rush, John Sutter bought the redwood-walled fort, whose buildings have recently been restored.

Fort Point
Golden Gate National Recreational Area, San Francisco
(415) 556-1693

This stoic reminder of the Civil War is dwarfed by the Golden Gate Bridge. The brick fortress, designed to protect the Golden Gate, contains some interesting war-time relics.

Sutter's Fort
28th and L streets, Sacramento
(916) 445-4209

Probably California's most famous fort, John Sutter's Sacramento settlement was the state's first community of settlers of European ancestry. Hand-held wands provide narration along a self-guided tour of rooms and buildings that portray life during California's early days.

Vikingsholm Castle
Emerald Bay, Lake Tahoe

It's a bit of a walk (the return trip uphill is the worst) but well worth the effort. The lakeside "castle," one of the nation's finest examples of Scandinavian architecture, is reminiscent of a Nordic fortress. It has three dozen or so rooms and a growing sod roof. Open for tours in the summer.

Scotty's Castle
Death Valley National Monument (north)
(619) 786-2331

No, it's not the desert playing tricks on your eyes. That's really a castle out there. Walter (Death Valley Scotty) Scott poured millions into this Spanish/Moorish vacation retreat, still decorated with expensive art and furnishings.

Fort Tejon
Off Interstate 5, south of Bakersfield
(805) 248-6692

Built in the mid-1800's, Fort Tejon had a short active life, protecting Southern California from 1854 to 1864. However, the barracks, headquarters, officers' quarters and other portions of the fort have been preserved. Civil War battle reenactments take place here frequently.

Riding the Rails

❦ The railroad grew up with California, but few of our children are growing up with the railroad. Once a vital form of passenger transportation, the train seems headed toward the endangered species list.

Fortunately, there are still several places up and down the state where folks can board (or at least look at) a restored steam train or vintage passenger car.

Some trains operate seasonally. Make sure you call first for times and specific directions. All aboard!

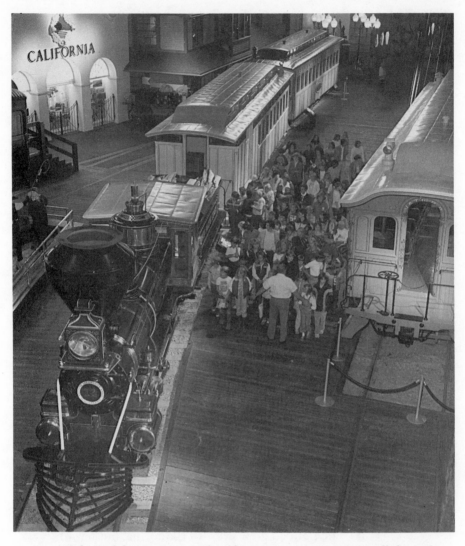

At the California State Railroad Museum, visitors can stroll through a clattering sleeper car, walk under a train weighing many tons, and view the rolling stock that helped shape the west.

Redwood Coast Railway Company: Willits to Eureka
299 East Commercial Street, Willits
(800) 482-7100

From Willits, the *North Coast Daylight* passes through miles of redwood forest, along the beautiful Eel River and the eastern shore of Humboldt Bay, arriving at Old Town, Eureka. The trip is 145 miles.

The Skunks: Willits to Fort Bragg
Main and Laurel, Fort Bragg
(707) 964-6371

The famous California Western Railroad "Skunk" trains run between Fort Bragg, on the north coast, and Willits, inland on Highway 101. Although you can spend close to eight hours on a 40-mile round-trip, shorter (four-hour) excursions operate between Willits and Northspur.

Roaring Camp and Big Trees Railroad
Graham Hill Road, Felton, in the Santa Cruz Mountains
(408) 335-4400

Old, steam-belching locomotives pull open flat cars up North America's steepest narrow-gauge grade through lush redwood forests as well as to and from from the city of Santa Cruz. Open all year.

Yosemite Mt. Sugar Pine Railroad
Fish Camp, near south entrance to Yosemite
(209) 683-7273

Take a four-mile scenic tour of the Sierra National Forest. You'll pass locales like Honey Hill Junction, Horseshoe Curve and Slab Creek. There are quaint Model A–powered rail cars and a logger steam train. The "Moonlight Special" run includes a barbeque dinner.

Westside and Cherry Valley Railway
Tuolumne-Sonora Road, Tuolumne City
(209) 928-4282

This rambling park features antique vehicle and boat rides as well as rides aboard the old Westside Flume and Lumber Company train.

Western Railway Museum
Highway 12, Suisun City
(10 miles east of Fairfield)
(707) 374-2978

Ride four different antique railway cars and rediscover the Art Deco flair of an old Pullman car. Steam engines operate occasionally. More than a hundred pieces of old rail equipment are displayed at this nonprofit, back-road museum.

Railtown 1897
Jamestown

More than a hundred movies and TV shows have been filmed on this railroad, whose tracks cover 12 miles of oak-studded hills. Unfortunately, this is an on-again, off-again attraction. In recent years, the historic trains have been idle more often than not. Although Railtown was closed at this writing, hopes were running high that the *Motherlode Cannonball* would run again. It's worth investigating if you find yourselves in the gold country. The depot is "downtown."

Train Town
Broadway, Sonoma
(707) 938-3912

This 15-minute ride is one of the shortest steam-train tours we've run across. Passengers get a quick taste of train travel, passing through 10 acres of forests, through a tunnel and over bridges.

Pacific Southwest Railway Museum: Camp to Clover Flats
La Mesa and Spring streets, La Mesa
(619) 465-8444 or
(619) 697-7762

During his second presidential campaign, Franklin Roosevelt used the museum-piece cars now on display here. Volunteers have restored the cars to their original elegance. A one-hour excursion train runs between Campo and Clover Flats.

California State Railroad Museum
Second and I streets, Old Sacramento
(916) 445-4209

Summer steam-train excursions run along the river out of a quaint depot in Old Sacramento. Nearby is America's finest interpretive railroad museum with numerous exquisitely restored locomotives and cars. This is a must-see for those with even the slightest interest in trains.

Orange Empire Railway Museum
South A Street, Perris (south of Riverside)
(714) 657-2605

Several pieces of rolling stock, from an old funeral car to city trolleys, have been preserved at this sprawling outdoor museum. Many of the cars are operational.

Underwater Worlds

🐚 When folks in America's heartland want to see fish up close they have to press their noses against their home aquariums. In California, we can feed a seal, get splashed by a killer whale or pet a bat ray.

Undersea World
Highway 101, Crescent City
(707) 464-3522

Displays at California's northernmost aquarium range from dangerous sea critters to tidepools.

Taylor Creek Stream Profile Chamber
Lake Tahoe Forest Visitor Center, Highway 89
(916) 544-6420

A sunken chamber with glass walls reveals rainbow trout swimming in a natural Sierra stream. In the fall, salmon dig in and defend their nests before your eyes.

Coyote Point Museum for Environmental Education
Coyote Point Park, San Mateo
(415) 342-7755

The aquarium at the small museum resembles a tidepool one might find along this part of the central coast.

Steinhart Aquarium
Golden Gate Park,
San Francisco
(415) 752-8268

The children will get a kick out of the alligators and crocodiles that inhabit a fountain area. More than two hundred tanks (most at kid's eye level) hold just about every type of water creature you could imagine, as well as the reptiles.

Among California museums with kid appeal, the Monterey Bay Aquarium is near the top of the list.

Long Marine Laboratory
Delaware Avenue, near the beach, Santa Cruz
(408) 429-4308

When UC Santa Cruz students aren't using the lab for research, it's open to the public. In addition to several living creatures, there's a skeleton of an 80-foot great blue whale.

Monterey Bay Aquarium
Cannery Row, Monterey
(408) 375-3333

This is the granddaddy of California's (probably America's) aquariums. The aquarium is home to some five thousand creatures, from sharks and sea otters to wolf eels and rock fish. There's a touch tidepool and a bat-ray petting pool, too.

Morro Bay Aquarium
595 Embarcadero, Morro Bay
(805) 772-7647

Inside the downtown gift shop
is an old aquarium with octopi,
eels and a preserved great white
shark. Visitors can also feed the
resident seals.

Cabrillo Marine Museum
Stephen White Drive, on the
beach, San Pedro
(213) 548-7562

Marine life of Southern California make their homes in
tidepools, mudflats and tanks.
Little ones won't be alarmed by
the sharks. They're less than
two feet long.

Scripps Aquarium
La Jolla Shores Drive, San Diego
(619) 452-6933

The public aquarium and
museum are part of the Scripps
Institute of Oceanography. Visitors get a lesson in wave action
and tidepools through special
displays. Some 150 marine species live here as well.

**Sea World, San Diego, and
Marine World Africa USA,
Vallejo**
See separate listings under
Part II of this book, on theme
parks.

Memorable Museums

❦ When I was a youngster, visiting a musty old museum with mom and dad ranked right up there with a trip to the barber or doctor. While California does have its share of museums that lean toward the esoteric, these 10 have definite kid appeal.

Wells Fargo History Museum
420 Montgomery Street,
San Francisco
(415) 396-2619

Climb aboard a stagecoach and tap out a message on the telegraph key. There's a similar museum at 444 S. Flower in Los Angeles.

Exploratorium
Palace of Fine Arts
3601 Lyon Street, San Francisco
(415) 563-7337

More than five hundred "please touch" interactive exhibits to dazzle little ears, eyes and hands.

Natural History Museum
Golden Gate Park,
San Francisco
(415) 752-8268

Whale skeletons, dinosaur bones, a moving "earthquake table" and a "Discovery Room" with hands-on exhibit highlight this part of the California Academy of Sciences. Also here are the Steinhart Aquarium and Morrison Planetarium.

Rosicrucian Egyptian Museum
Park and Naglee avenues,
San Jose
(408) 287-9171

Kids will likely want to push past the jewelry, scrolls and figurines for a look at real mummies and shrunken heads. A steel gate locks upon your entering a scale model of an Egyptian tomb.

California State Railroad Museum
Second and I streets,
Old Sacramento
(916) 445-4209

They didn't make museums like this when we were little. This spare-no-expense tribute to the train contains numerous lavishly restored locomotives and other "rolling stock" set against realistic dioramas.

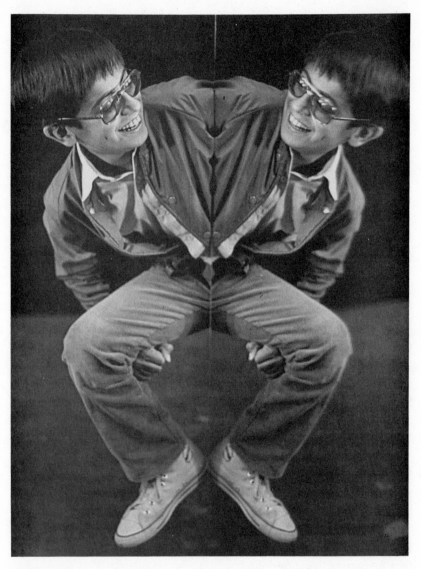

If you're bringing the kids to San Francisco, a visit to the Exploratorium is as important as a ride on the cable cars.

Kidspace
390 S. El Molino, Pasadena
(818) 449-9144

No stuffy "hands-off" exhibits
in this former school. Children
should be prepared to take con-
trol. They can try on grown-up
uniforms, crawl through an "ant
hill," meet a talking robot or
assemble the body organs of a
lifelike mannequin.

Hobby City Doll
and Toy Museum
1238 South Beach Boulevard,
Anaheim
(714) 527-2323

This one's easy to spot. It's a
half-scale replica of the White
House, and inside are dolls and
toys representing countries
from around the world. There
are more than 20 toy and craft-
type shops here, as well.

La Habra Children's Museum
301 S. Euclid Street, La Habra
(213) 694-1011

This kids' museum is located a
few miles north of Disneyland
in a former railroad depot.
Inside are a living bee observa-
tory, musical instruments, hulking stuffed animals and even an
exhibit that lets able-bodied
kids experience life with a
disability.

Los Angeles Children's Museum
301 N. Main Street, Los Angeles
(213) 687-8800

Young visitors might be over-
whelmed by the activities here.
They include a workshop where
household flotsam becomes
works of art, a dress-up area
with multicultural clothing and
a sprawling, plastic-brick con-
struction area.

Children's Museum of San
Diego
8657 Villa La Jolla Drive,
La Jolla
(619) 450-0767

This facility designed for the
young combines many of the
interactive displays and exhibits
found at the other south-state
children's museums, including
a doctor's office setup, TV studio and exhibits involving sen-
sory stimuli.

Fabulous Festivities

❦ When it comes to throwing a party, California knows how to do it right. From celebrations of garlic to antique air shows, there's always something going on in the state's big cities or little burgs. Here's a season-by-season listing of just a few of the Golden State's festivals of family fun.

WINTER

Chinese New Year
San Francisco
(415) 982-3000

Los Angeles
(213) 617-0396

Dragon parades, firecrackers, cultural programs and more.

Whale Festivals
Mendocino and Fort Bragg
(707) 964-3153

Spirit of the Whales, Dana Point
(714) 496-2274

Celebrate (and see) these mighty creatures during their annual migratory pass. Cioppino feeds, arts and crafts and a whale of a good time.

Christmas Celebrations
Victorian Christmas
Nevada City
(916) 265-2692

The streets of this quaint Gold Rush hamlet come alive with a Christmas fair, old-time costumes and lots of food.

Las Posadas
Olvera Street, Los Angeles
(213) 625-5045

This nine-day Mexican Christmas celebration is highlighted by nightly candlelight processions along the street.

SPRING

King Korn Karnival
Coachella
(619) 398-5111

Join Coachella Valley residents in celebrating their golden sweet-corn harvest.

Fiesta de la Primavera
San Diego
(714) 232-3101

Where else but Old Town San Diego can you find both mariachi bands and fiddlers?

Fourth of July Celebrations
Aptos and La Selva Beach
(408) 423-1111

These Santa Cruz County communities take pride in their community parades, which must rank among the nation's shortest. Games and goodies follow each.

Ventura
(805) 648-2075

In Ventura's similar parade, "floats" usually take the form of skateboards and streamer-laden wagons.

Gravenstein Apple Fair
Ragle Ranch Park
Sebastopol, Sonoma County
(707) 996-1090

In addition to plenty of apple foods and desserts, this folksy celebration offers activities for kids including storytellers, puppet shows and a petting zoo.

Garlic Festival
Gilroy (south of San Jose)
(408) 842-1625

Gilroy, hands-down the world's garlic capital, celebrates this spicy product (in everything from ice cream to perfume) at an odoriferous weekend food fest that draws hundreds of thousands of folks. (Pick up your mouthwash on the way out.)

FALL

Art and Pumpkin Festival
Half Moon Bay (south of
San Francisco)
(415) 726-9652

Children wade through acres and acres of coastal pumpkin patches in search of that special one. This is also the site of the "Great Pumpkin Weigh-Off."

Begonia Festival
Capitola (Santa Cruz County)
(408) 423-1111

The highlight of this popular annual celebration is a nautical parade where the floats really float. There's also a sand-castle-building contest on Capitola Beach that's open to pros and amateurs alike.

Pismo Beach Clam Festival

Pismo Beach (south of San Luis Obispo)
(805) 773-4382

This is a clam lover's paradise. You can dig for them and taste them in all sorts of gastronomic delights.

Fall Harvest Festival

Julian (east of San Diego)
(619) 765-1857

This rustic southern foothill town holds an annual back-road festival that includes entertainment, apple foods and art show.

California Cruising

❦ You've driven over the Golden Gate Bridge, but have you sailed under her? You've gazed out over Lake Tahoe, but have you cruised her pristine shoreline? Maybe you've seen the tall buildings of San Diego from the street, but have you experienced the city skyline from the bay?

Next time you visit one of California's coastal cities or inland lakes, park the car for an hour or two and hop aboard a tour boat (or even a houseboat) for a fresh perspective – from the water.

Humboldt Bay Harbor Cruise

Departs from the foot of
C Street, Eureka
(707) 442-3738 or 445-1910

From mid-June through mid-September, the M.V. *Madaket* cruises one of California's most scenic bays.

Shasta Lake Cruise

Departs Bridge Bay Marina, north of Redding off Interstate 5
(916) 275-3021

One of California's newest sternwheelers, the *Bridge Bay Belle*, runs two-hour cruises along Shasta's hilly shoreline, past the dam and up the McCloud River to Lake Shasta Caverns.

From its south shore berth, the Tahoe Queen *paddles the emerald waters of its namesake lake.*

Lake Tahoe Cruises

The *Tahoe Queen* Glass Bottom Boat
Departs from the foot of Ski Run Boulevard, South Lake Tahoe
(916) 541-3364

The M.S. *Dixie*
Departs from Zephyr Cove Marina, south shore (Nevada side)
(702) 588-3508

These two venerable paddle-wheelers follow similar courses on the lake offering unob-structed forest and Sierra views. Emerald Bay, with tiny Fannette Island and Vikingsholm Castle, is the highlight of the Tahoe cruise. The two boats compete in the annual six-mile Great Lake Tahoe Sternwheeler Race on Memorial Day weekend.

San Francisco Bay Cruises

The Red and White Fleet
Departs from Piers 41 and 43½
(800) 445-8880

The Blue and Gold Fleet
Departs from Pier 39's west
marina
(415) 781-7877

The Red and White Fleet's more
than half-dozen cruises include
the Golden Gate and the Bay;
Alcatraz (walking or cruise-
around tours); Angel Island and
Tiburon (ferry service – bring
your bikes); and Marine World
Africa USA.

The Blue and Gold vessels
cruise past all of the city's
major landmarks, as well as
Angel Island, Alcatraz and
quaint Tiburon. You'll also pass
under the Golden Gate and Bay
bridges.

Northern California Houseboating

The California Delta and Lake
Shasta are the most popular
state waterways for family
houseboating. The Delta has
some thousand miles of navi-
gable waterways, and Shasta,
California's largest lake, has
more than three hundred miles
of shoreline.

If the children are water-safe,
this is a good way to get re-
acquainted with the family;
unless you jump overboard
you'll be sharing very close
quarters. Most houseboats
(there are many different "floor-
plans") come with a full galley
(kitchen) and lots of space for
sleeping, but few separate
rooms.

The California Office of
Tourism publishes a listing of
houseboat rental agencies for
Shasta, the Delta, Lake Don
Pedro, Lake Berryessa and other
California bodies of water.
Request a copy by writing the
office at 1121 L Street, Suite
103, Sacramento, CA 95814.
Telephone (916) 322-1396.

Sacramento River Cruises
Departs Old Sacramento
waterfront
(916) 441-6481

The *Matthew McKinley*, an 82-foot paddlewheeler, follows a route well known to Gold Rush prospectors who made their way from San Francisco upriver to the gold fields via Sacramento's historic waterfront.

Morro Bay Cruise
Departs from the Morro Bay
Embarcadero
(805) 772-2257 or 772-2255

The sternwheeler *Tigers Folly II* takes visitors to the south-central coast on hour-long cruises past huge Morro Rock, along the entrance to the harbor and along the Embarcadero.

Channel Islands National Park Cruises
Departs Ventura and Oxnard
harbors
(805) 642-1393

Day-long adventures to this new national park include a visit to Anacapa, a wild, undeveloped island with tidepools and trails. Shorter, cruise-only excursions are offered for those not interested in landing on the island.

San Diego Harbor Cruises
Harbor Excursions
Departs from foot of Broadway
(619) 233-6872

Two-hour harbor tours take in the largest Navy fleet in the continental U.S.

Bahia Belle
Departs from Mission Bay
(619) 488-0551

This Victorian sternwheeler stays within Mission Bay between three hotels, including the San Diego Princess (which is recommended as a resort destination in Part I).

Invader Cruises
Depart from the Embarcadero at Harbor
(619) 298-8066

Choose between a paddle-wheeler and a schooner for a two-hour tour of the harbor.

Top Tours

❦ Take a behind-the-scenes tour and learn how they make everything from coins to chocolate.

Shasta Dam
Highway 15, off Interstate 5
north of Redding

See how this second-highest dam in the world really works (self-guided tour).

California Cooperative Creamery
Western and Baker streets
Petaluma
Tour a real cheese factory.
(707) 778-1234

Uncle Gaylord's
824 Petaluma Boulevard
Petaluma
(707) 778-6008

See how they make ice cream and cookies in this sweet-treat factory (free samples).

Marin French Cheese Company (tasting included)
On Novato Boulevard at Point Reyes–Petaluma Road, Marin County
(707) 762-6001

Sonoma Cheese Factory
(self-guided)
2 Spanish Street
Sonoma
(707) 966-1000

Loleta Cheese Factory
252 Loleta Drive, Loleta
(707) 733-5470

Alcatraz Prison
San Francisco Bay
Reservations: telephone
(415) 392-7469

Walk the halls and visit a cell in this infamous prison, former home of Al Capone and Machine Gun Kelly. Tours leave Pier 41 in San Francisco.

The Old U.S. Mint
Fifth and Mission streets,
San Francisco
(415) 974-0788

Ninety-minute tours of this 1906 earthquake survivor include restored rooms and a close look at a fortune in gold bullion.

Hershey Chocolate Company
1400 S. Yosemite Avenue,
Oakdale (near Modesto)
(209) 847-0381

Just like Willy Wonka's Chocolate Factory, this is where they make kisses, candy bars and chocolate sauce. Tours leave every 30 minutes. Tastings included.

California Almond Growers
Visitor Center
17th and C streets, Sacramento
(916) 446-8439

Ever wonder what happens to almonds between picking and packaging? Wonder no more. Noisy machines, a mile-long conveyor and huge storage bins are part of this tour. Tastings included.

Los Angeles Times
202 W. First Street, Los Angeles
(213) 972-5757

The nation's largest-circulation standard-size daily newspaper offers one-hour tours that cover the newsroom to the pressroom.

Eagle Mine
C Street, Julian
(619) 765-9921

Daily tours take visitors deep underground to experience life in the mines. The tour culminates with an opportunity to pan for gold.

San Diego Wild Animal Park
15500 San Pasqual Valley Road, Escondido
(619) 231-1515

Take the two-mile "Walk on the Wild Side" for a look at food warehouses, lion and tiger bedrooms and a lesson in how breeding programs work. Regular tours (described in Part II) don't cover this part of the park. Bring your comfy walking shoes.

Bates Brothers Nut Farm
15954 Woods Valley Road, Valley Center
(619) 749-3333

This produce processing plant and store are 40 miles north of San Diego. In addition to a tour of the plant, visitors will enjoy the farm animals and picnic area.

Index

About the Author

Bill Gleeson is a fourth-generation Californian who, with his wife and two children, has covered several thousand miles of highways and byways in search of family-oriented travel destinations. Gleeson is also the author of *Backroad Wineries of California* and *Small Hotels of California*, both for Chronicle Books. His stories about and photographs of California appear frequently in state and national publications.

When they're not on the road, the Gleesons make their home in Northern California.